Fourth Revised Edition

MANUAL OF PRACTICAL COLON CLASSIFICATION

By the Same Author

- ★ Exercises in the 19th Edition of the Dewey Decimal Classification
- ★ Sears-16: Sears List of Subject Headings: A Practical Introduction for Indian Students

---

About the Author

Mohinder Partap Satija is a librarian and library science teacher of 30 years experience. He has authored 25 books, 110 papers, 150 book reviews published in India and abroad, and has contributed papers to national and international (FID, IFLA, ISKO) conferences. He has visited Germany, England, Finland, and the Netherlands in connection with his professional work. In some of his books and papers he has collaborated with internationally known experts. He is associated with library journals such as Information Management Report (Bowker-Saur) , Library Times International (USA), Lucknow Librarian (India), Ranganathan Research Bulletin (India) and Knowledge Organization (Germany).

Mr. Satija obtained his Ph.D. on Ranganathan Studies and is currently a Professor in Guru Nanak Dev University, Amritsar.

MANUAL OF PRACTICAL COLON CLASSIFICATION

(Fourth Revised Edition)

MP SATIJA
Guru Nanak Dev University

CONCEPT PUBLISHING COMPANY, NEW DELHI-110059

ISBN 81-7022-971-5 (PB)

First Edition, 1984

Second Revised Edition, 1989

Third Revised Edition, 1995

Fourth Revised Edition, 2002

Published and Printed by
Ashok Kumar Mittal
Concept Publishing Company
A/15-16, Commercial Block, Mohan Garden
NEW DELHI-110059 (India)

Phones: 5648039, 5649024
Fax: 091-11-5648053
Email: publishing@conceptpub.com

Lovingly Dedicated
To

P S G KUMAR

A model librarian, and teacher
An inspiring colleague

PREFACE TO THE FOURTH EDITION

Continued teaching of the Colon Classification, sixth edition (CC-6, 1963) in library schools prompts us to keep this *Manual* in print by bringing its another edition. Over the last decade there has been an unprecedented (and regretfully unwanted and unwieldy, too) expansion of library education in India, especially in distance education sector. This situation calls for a further simplification of the book without compromising on its standards. Accordingly the already lucid text has been simplified and made more explicit here and there. Some new class numbers for current subjects have been added. Chapter on book number has been restored in a concise and simplified version. Hope the students and teachers find the new edition useful, as earlier. Endeavour is to keep the *Manual* relevant and current despite the new chronic handicaps of the CC-6 system. Emphasis of the *Manual* is still on to be a self-sufficient workbook for the beginners as well as the advance students.

Thanks are to Paivi Pekkarinen, a Ranganathan scholar, for her interest in this book and suggestions for its improvement. Thanks to Ashok Mittal for ensuring its availability to the student community; and above all to the students and teachers for their encouraging response. Suggestions for its improvement will be thankfully acknowledged.

Dipawali 2001

M.P. SATIJA
satija_mp@yahoo.com

PREFACE TO THE THIRD EDITION

The seventh edition of the Colon Classification was at last published in 1987, but the classifiers and the library schools have opted to continue with the sixth edition (reprint 1963). Therefore, it continues to be the popular and stable edition. The sixth edition is the representative of the Colon Classification system.

Since its first publication in 1984, the *Manual of Practical Colon Classification* has been used as a class text in many Indian library schools throughout the country. There has been a demand for its translation in various Indian languages, even. Many unknown students and fellow teachers have commended the book for its details and lucidity. In this edition misprints have been corrected. Some new examples have been added. The Preface to the first edition though bit outdated has been retained for its historical value. Feedback from the users is solicited again. It will help to refine the *Manual* further and make it continuously and more useful.

M.P. SATIJA

PREFACE

Reputation has always played a trick on Ranganathan's Colon Classification—or like Janus it is two-faced. Theorywise it is world famous, but there are many who have not yet even seen a copy of its schedules. There are many who draw intellectual pleasure in building CC numbers, while many more are deterred by its minute details. To some its dexterity in providing minutely co-extensive class numbers is mentally stimulating, while others are benumbed by the complexity of its devices and rules. On the average, librarians are afraid of learning it, as they grantedly take it a difficult scheme to learn and apply. It is a fear which is based on more hearsay rather than on self-experiences. At the same time it may be admitted that all the fears are not unjustified. Many factors conspire to give it the semblance of a difficult scheme. We have been hesitating to learn it, that is the predominant hurdle in the way of its popularity. Other factors impeding its widespread use have been discussed at length, in the library literature, more than once.[1]

In the beginning there has been a dearth of books explaining the intricacies of the scheme. The Rule part of the schedule contains so many illustrations and detailed guidance that it mostly obviates the need for any guidebook. Therefore, I still maintain that the best guide (and authentic, too) to learn CC is CC itself. No other guide can equal its clarity and depth. But some students, perhaps psychologically, depend upon secondary explanatory material. To fulfil the needs of such students K.M. Sivaraman, Ranganathan's close associate, and head of the classification section of the Madras University library wrote a book on the practical aspects of the CC in 1943. Inevitably that book had Ranganathan's approval but remained mostly in obscurity for reasons not too far to know. Ranganathan wrote another such book by himself, which contained 1008 examples : *Library Classification : Fundamentals and Procedures* (1944). The book is now totally dated: Ranganathan, in spite of his announcements, could not bring out a second edition of the book. Ranganathan's other books on classification such as *Elements of Library Classification* (1962), *A Descriptive Account of Colon Classification* (1965) and the *Prolegomena to Library Classification*

1. For example see Maltby, Arthur, *Sayers' Manual of Classification for Librarians*, 5th ed., London, Andre Deutsch, 1975, pp. 201-203.

(1967), help to some extent in understanding the scheme, though it is something beyond their scope.

After the publication of the sixth edition (1960) of the scheme, books began to appear expounding the techniques of number building in Colon Classification. Ironically, the first such book came from abroad, viz. C.D., Batty's *An Introduction to Colon Classification* (1966). After this there seems a small spurt of books aiming to familiarise the students with Colon Classification. Books by Bhargava and Sood (1975), O.P. Uppal (1975), Ajoy Mukhopadhyaya (1976), M.P. Chand (1978), P.S.G. Kumar (1979), M.S. Sachdeva (1976, 1980), Navalani and Gidwani (1981), and Khanna and Kapil (1982) present a colourful variety to suit different minds and pockets.[2] This outspurt of books is explainable by two factors. Firstly, by this time the scheme had become a vital part of the syllabi for B.Lib. Sc. and M.Lib. Sc. studies in almost all the Indian universities. Abroad, it was being introduced as a species of advanced classification based on facet analysis and synthesis principles. For this reason more minds became engaged in study and research of the scheme. Secondly, it was also thought that the scheme (after the sixth edition) has reached a stabilized phase and consequently, transcended the frequently revisiting circle of drastic revisions and amendments. Such hopes were belied by the changes announced for the seventh edition. Even the 1963 Annexure of the sixth edition contained disturbing changes.

It was a time when its reputat:on was all time high. But the tantalizing delay in publishing the seventh edition has cast on it a shadow of aging. Notwithstanding the repeated announcements since the first year of the previous decade, no new edition has come yet. It is fast becoming obsolete in contents. In the face of the unprecedented growth of knowledge its potent devices too seem helpless in coping with the sea tide of literature. It looks senile and feeble bodily.

But its methods have pervaded classification. Therefore, its methods, and in this guise the CC itself, will survive as long as all that goes by the name of classification survives. Its techniques and theory provide guidelines and stepping stones for other schemes. New schemes being devised, especially the special subject schemes, are mostly faceted in nature.[3] A major success came to the CC camp when in the Dorking Conference (1957) faceted classification was agreed overwhelmingly as the most helpful classification for a dynamic universe of knowledge.[4] DDC, after its 16th edition, has gradually introduced the synthesis

2. Satija, M.P. and Amrik Singh : *A Bibliography of Colon Classification, 1930-1993*, New Delhi : M.D. Publications, 1994.
3. Maltby, Arthur, *Sayers' Manual of Classification for Librarians*, 5th ed., London, Andre Deutsch, 1975, pp. 302-303.

method. UDC has absorbed some of its very specific methods and some terminology as well. BC2, revised by J Mills, has widely employed the method of synthesis through its retroactive notation. Even the BSO to be used for the UNISIST programme, and which is the latest entry in the world of general schemes, is faceted in nature. A faceted scheme has been found more amenable to computers. Many thesauri, for example, Thesaurofacet by J. Aitchison and her team, are based on facet principles. CC has been a pioneer in formulating subject indexing languages (SIL) : Chain Indexing, thesaurofacet, POPSI and now the Classarus are all based on it. PRECIS is just a refined modification of Chain Indexing. In nutshell, it is an age of faceted classifications and the enumerative schemes are now of historical interest only. The worldwide interest in faceted schemes culminated in B.C. Vickery's *Faceted Classification : A Guide to Construction and Use of Special Schemes*, Aslib, London 1960. Thus, the spirit of CC is still young and rejuvenates itself every now and then in new vestures. The scheme, therefore, is no more as different and unique as it used to be. Its terminology has been adopted in the general theory of classification, as well as in other schemes. In this way awful halo of complexity it was wearing is gradually vanishing. But it is still an exemplary general scheme based on Facet Analysis. It is still sufficiently unique to maintain its individuality. Its theory and applications still demand considerably arduous efforts for learning.

In the CC itself there are some ambiguous and obscure rules, which have not sufficiently been illustrated even by Ranganathan himself. Therefore, such rules look hazy and obfuscating. Different authors have interpreted them in different ways, though a scientific rule has no room for varied interpretations. If it has happened here, Ranganathan has no less part of the blame to bear. Errors, misprints, equivocal rules, self-contradictions, statements less than adequate, rules *sans* examples, still swarm the pages of the CC schedules. No official clarifications have been given publicly. It discounts the popularity and accuracy of the scheme. The present book is not any endeavour to keep the scheme alive from the ravages of time. It seems tied to a dying animal in the guise of the sixth edition : and death is coming by slow degrees to it. Nothing short of a new edition can help to keep the scheme in the mainstream. And a widespread learning of the scheme is necessary to make it a part of librarian's lore.

The book in hand, *A Manual of Practical Colon Classification*, aims to expound with ample illustrations every rule big and small through a combing operation. Illustrations are a major feature of the

4. Atherton, Pauline, ed., *Classification Research : Proceedings of the Elsinore Conference*, Denmark, 1964; Copenhagen, Munksgaard, 1965, pp. 111-113.

book. It delves deep into the rules, so is likely to be helpful to the advanced students. Yet, no background knowledge has been assumed on the part of readers: an attempt has been made to make it self-sufficient. Therefore, it is equally helpful for the beginners. Use of technical terminology has been kept to the minimum. The introduction for this purpose has been written afresh. It may also help to understand and illustrate the theory of the CC, though this role has been subordinated. The main purpose of the book is to help the Colon Classification students to understand, especially some obscure rules. It is a student-oriented book.

To serve as a textbook, this manual has been patterned. In the first part fundamental principles, and devices have been given a chapter each. The part second allots a chapter each to a main class recognised by the scheme. These chapters deal particularly with the peculiarities and exceptional rules of the individual main classes. Each chapter on an individual main class also contains examples illustrating the use of common isolates, phase relation, various devices and parallel schedules. This kind of repetition is deliberate and a recurring feature of this book. It is a sort of drill with the objective of naturalizing the learners, without conscious efforts, in the obscure terrains of the scheme. Exercises for the students have not been given. But the large number of solved examples will obviate the need for such exercises. Most of the examples in the *Manual* are imaginary, rather than a part of the literary warrant. It has been a forced necessity to depict the versatility of the rules and to exhibit their use in full play. It is also a warning that the *Manual* may not help much the Colon practitioners in solving their day to day problems. Now there are many familiar topics having no assigned places in the scheme. As said earlier, CC as it stands in 1980's is severely handicapped waiting a revision. Genuine difficulties of the classifiers of this scheme are mounting everyday. No effort has been done here to assuage such difficulties. M.P. Chand has tried to solve such problems on the basis of his personal correspondence with Ranganathan. This book strictly confines itself to the framework of the CC schedules. It is a book on number building rather than on classification. But within these confines creativity has not been curbed. Many fabricated examples of unenumerated subjects, but obtainable through the devices, have been provided only to show the creativity of the scheme. Titles are mostly imaginary: the solutions, it is hoped, are factual. Here, only an attempt has been made to show what we can do with CC : what we cannot do has not been spoken of. To be thorough, deep, well illustrated and lucid have been the objectives and *raison d'ētre* of writing the book.

June 1984 M.P. SATIJA

CONTENTS

THEORETICAL PRINCIPLES

0

THE STRUCTURE OF THE TEXT OF COLON CLASSIFICATION

The Colon Classification (CC) first designed from 1924 to 1928 and published first in 1933 by the Madras Library Association is now in its 7th edition released in 1987. The sixth edition (CC-6), still the most popular one, was published in 1960. A reprint with some amendments contained in an annexure was issued in 1963. This *Manual* aiming to be a guide to the use of CC-6, explains the construction of (Compound and Complex) class numbers by this edition (1963) which was reprinted in 1964 and 1969 by its publishers Asia Publishing House Bombay. Since 1989 this edition with annexure has been reprinted many times by the Sarada Ranganathan Endowment for Library Science.* This text has the following bibliographical details:

> S R Ranganathan : Colon Classification, 6th ed.: basic Classification. Bangalore : Sarada Ranganathan Endowment, 1989 (reprinted many times later). 28+1.124+2.172+3.126 p. ISBN 81-85 273-31-6.

The entire text is in three constituent parts preceded by 1-28 prefatory pages including an annexure (pp. 19-28) containing important amendments and corrections. It is advisable to carry out these corrections and changes at appropriate pages in the rules and schedules. The three basic parts of the text are :

Part 1	Rules	pp. 1.1 to 1.124
Part 2	Schedules of Classification	pp. 2.1 to 2.172
Part 3	Schedules of Classics, etc.	pp. 3.1 to 3.126

* It is a trust founded by Ranganathan at Bangalore in 1965 in honour of his wife Sarada Ranganathan (1908-1985) to promote study and research in library and information sciences. The Endowment is legal heir to Ranganathan's intellectual and material property.

Part 1 defines basic concepts and provides rules for constructing class numbers in general and for each main class individually. It comprises of three kinds of chapters: Chapters preceded by Zero, viz., 01 to 08 (pp. 1.1 to 1.40) which explain the basic terminology and general principles of Ranganathan's system of classification. Chapter 1 to 8 (pp. 1.41 to 1.61) explain common general rules and peripheral appendages to a class number : and rules for constructing isolate numbers for various components of a compound and complex class numbers. The chapters 9z to Z (pp. 1.62 to 1.122) explain one by one rules exclusive to each of the main class of the CC-6, and other oddities in the facet formula of each main class. Each rule has been given a mnemonic number. At the end is an index to concepts and terms (pp. 1.123-1.124).

Part 2 contains chapterwise schedules of various common isolates, common categories of space and time and special isolates of different main classes from z to Z. Each main class has first been divided into canonical classes, if existing, and further into isolates divided under [P] [M], [E] formatted into arrays and chains. Systems and specials, if any, are given at the end of each main class.

In this part there are four indexes :

1. Geographical index (pp. 2.18 to 2.25);
2. Botany : index to natural groups (pp. 2.16 to 2.63);
3. Zoology : index to natural groups (pp. 2.73 to 2.78);
4. General index to isolates under all common schedules and main classes. [See Chapter 10 (pp. 78-80)] of this *Manual*.

Part 3 comprises of two sections : the first section lists in a classified order readymade class numbers for various classics mainly in Indology. The second section is an alphabetical index to the classics with its class number against each. This part is useful to the working librarians for classifying their collections by the CC.

There is a parallelism in all the three parts, e.g., Chapter P in Part 1 provides rules for constructing class numbers in P linguistics (pp. 1.105-1.107); in part 2 chapter P contains a schedule of isolates, and Part 3 chapter P (pp. 3.14 to 3.21) provides readymade class numbers for Indian classics in P Linguistics. Chapter numbers have only ordinal value rather than any serial number. Each part has its own page numbering; and each page is given a serial number preceded by part number, e.g., 2.134 means page number 134 in Part 2, and so on. A consolidated table of contents for all the three parts has been given at page 7.

1

THE STRUCTURE OF THE SYSTEM

This book explains class number building by the CC Sixth edition (1963). The CC is a general scheme which aims to classify by subject all kinds of documents—books, periodicals, reports, pamphlets, microforms and electronic media in all kinds of libraries. For bibliographic records, requiring depth classification, it is especially suitable. S.R. Ranganathan (1892-1972), its author, was a mathematician, before he embraced librarianship as a profession in 1924. He encountered the Dewey Decimal Classification scheme while learning library science in the school of library science, University College, London. At the first blush the scheme appeared not only inadequate or a defunct tool for knowledge organisation but also seemed founded on unscientific principles—rather on no principle, (Its absence of any theoretical background is admitted even by its designers, who call it a pragmatic scheme). With the DDC Ranganathan was able to assign two numbers to most of the books, thus defeating the very purpose of classification itself. Besides this, Ranganathan also found only a nominal representation of Indian subjects in the scheme.

All these factors prompted Ranganathan to devise an ideal scheme free of all such defects. Ranganathan based his scheme, which he named Colon Classification, not only on his full cognizance of the shortcomings of the then existing schemes, but also on the of literary warrant and trends in emergence of new subjects. Since documents are nothing but the embodiment of knowledge, so knowledge is librarian's stock in trade. Understanding of the ways of growth of knowledge is vital for a classificationist. Ranganathan's studies on the growth of knowledge have been recognized as a valuable contribution to the library science. He studied minutely the ways in which knowledge grows and new subjects emerge; and applied this knowledge in designing and developing his scheme.

The Colon Classification presumes the entire body of universal knowledge woven in a system: vis-a-vis, sees an underlying unity in it. All knowledge is one, he learned from the *Vedas*. In its mapping of the knowledge, the structure that ultimately emerges out from the CC is both traditional and revolutionary at once. The fact that Ranganathan recognizes and honours the existence of time-honoured main and canonical classes, makes his scheme look steeped in tradition. His scheme is described as Analytico-Synthetic, which implies that the scheme does not go in for making an exhaustive list of all possible subjects known at that time, as was usually done in those days. The first division of the universe of knowledge is into traditional main classes, but in between Ranganathan has interposed what he calls *partially comprehensive main classes:* Mathematical Sciences, Biological Sciences, Humanities are examples of such classes. The main classes, therefore, are removed twice from the universe of knowledge taken as a unified whole. Main classes, wherever possible, have been divided into *canonical classes.*[1] At this juncture the scheme makes a clean break with the past. It diverges radically from every other scheme. Instead of carrying forward that mode of division to the extent possible, Ranganathan divides main or canonical class into the *Five Fundamental Categories* by applying simultaneously the five characteristics of division.[2] The Five Fundamental Categories are namely *Personality, Matter, Energy, Space* and *Time* in their decreasing order of concreteness, popularly known by the initionym PMEST. A fundamental category is divided into *facets*, and facets into *isolates*. In CC an isolate is the ultimate unit of knowledge. Here lies his originality.

Subject Analysis

Determination of the Main Class

To assign a Colon Class number to any given subject, the first step is to analyse the title into its constituent fundamental categories. But even prior to this, the main class to which the subject falls must be determined as the categories exist within the framework of main or canonical classes, not of the partially comprehensive classes or the universe of knowledge direct. The CC is a very standardised scheme, so every subject/title belongs to one and only one main class.[3] This is also in accordance with his Canon of Homonym.[4] In every scheme contents of a main class are settled by enumeration only, otherwise, no formula can help. Similarly, nothing helps to determine the main class of a subject except one's wide familiarity with the scheme and its layout. Ranganathan defines a main class as "an organised or systematised body of ideas whose extension and intention are likely to fall coherently within the field of interest and comfortably within the intellectual competence and the field of inevitable specialisation of a normal person". But this is not any helpful definition. Ranganathan admits that main class of a "subject will have to be determined by Trial and Error".[5] Thus some flair and practice may lessen the difficulties by and by.

Analysis into Fundamental Categories

After determining the main class of a subject, the job of breaking a given subject into its constituent categories is more than half the game. It is no exaggeration to call it the very essence of analysis. These fundamental categories are not as difficult to be identified as it is to define them. Categories tend to evade all definitions. We know what they mean: but cannot tell what they are. A paradox. It is due to lack of experience. For example, the category Personality occurs in all the main classes, but to say with certainty that it is such and such is very difficult, indeed. Only experience helps to recognise the categories. Reflex action or flair based on experience may also help. Nevertheless, they are best defined by enumeration. To some extent they are intuitive, too. Therefore, if something puzzles us, the only answer seems that either we should acquire Ranganathan's intuitive insight, or acquiesce the way Ranganathan desired.

Ranganathan slowly developed from 1928 to 1952 the concept of *Five Fundamental Categories* (FFC) of knowledge. His concept of fundamental categories is comparable to any great theory of the order of what A. Kuhn calls paradigms. The basis of the fundamental categories concept seems to be the recurring symmetry in the whole body of knowledge which in turn is transmitted to the coherent fragments called the main classes. It is a hypothesis that every idea, every subject is manifestation of one or more (at the most five) categories. It has been postulated by Ranganathan that there are Five and only Five Fundamental Categories—Personality, Matter, Energy, Space and Time. It means that in the CC the recurrence of the fundamental categories is exactly in the manner a chemist recognizes every kind of matter in any form, constituent of any or some of the 104 basic chemical elements. The hypothesis of Five Fundamental Categories (FFC) is only a working assumption. Nevertheless, the number of categories has been challenged. It is vulnerable, no doubt. The number of categories depends on how you define a category. The idea of categories in epistemology is as old as Aristotle. In between many philosophers have pondered on the problem and aired their views. But the discussion of categories in bibliographic (or library) classification came only after the introduction of the idea by Ranganathan and later by other faceteers and faceted schemes of classification on Ranganathan's pattern. Many librarians, such as B.C. Vickery, D.J. Foskett, J. Mills, D.W. Langridge and other CRG members have constructed many faceted special subject schemes on the assumption of varying number of categories. Anyhow, it is admitted that so far only he has given the least number of categories. Ranganathan's assumption is working well, that is all.

Array and Chains

In the process of division, each category is first divided into facets. A *facet* is the totality of divisions of a category based on a single train of characteristics. In the facet formula every train of characteristics is enclosed within square brackets.[6] Each facet is a finely patterned web of *arrays* and *chains*. The first division is into arrays by applying different trains of characteristics. An *array* is a sequence of entities of equal rank. All the main classes form an array. Take a homely example, all the children of a parent form a single array. In a class numbers, within a facet all the entities denoted by equal number of digits form an array. For example, in the chapter of language isolates (page 2.26), the isolate number 1, 2, 3, 4, 5, 6, 7, 8, 9 form an array. Another array is denoted by 11, 12, 13, 14, 15, 16. Every link in the array is divided into ultimate divisions which are arranged in a chain. A *chain* is thus defined as a sequence of isolates in successive subordination. Take again the example from the schedule of language isolates (page 2.26), the entities bearing the isolate numbers 1, 11 and 111 form a chain. Similarly 1, 15, 151, 1511 form another chain. Giving a homely example, a family lineage constitutes a chain. Thus grandfather, father, son, and grandson form a family chain. Science, Physics, Heat, Thermodynamics form a chain of subjects.

An isolate is the ultimate division of knowledge in the CC. Isolates are to the CC what the words are to a language. In a given context an isolate belongs to one and only one facet, thus to one category and one main class only. Isolates are of two kinds special and common, depending upon their jurisdiction—area over which these are applicable. Special isolates belong only to a main class, while the applicability of the common isolates is universal. Common isolates can be applied to any main class; any class number. This, however, will be taken later for detailed considerations.

Identification of Categories

Of the five categories, the last two, *viz.*, Space and Time are recurring, so they are the common categories. They remain the same whatsoever may be the subject, therefore, have been enumerated once for all at pages 2.18 to 2.17, and 2.7 respectively.

The sequence PMEST is in the decreasing order of concreteness: [P] is the most concrete and least abstract; [T] is the most abstract and least concrete. But paradoxically the [P], though most concrete, is relatively difficult to be identified. On the other hand [T] though most abstract is the most easy to be identified in a given subject. Therefore, in practical classification, we start from the [T] and come down to [P] *via* SEM.

Time

Obviously it is the chronological factor in a subject. 21st century poetry, medieval science, economic progress in the last decade, or the 2002 Presidential Elections, all these subjects involve the time facet. In the CC the provision is to represent time up to a particular year, for example, "Political Events in 1980". But we cannot indicate a particular month or day. Seasonal and diurnal time as winter, snow, day, night can be denoted. Thus the provisions to indicate time very precisely, are more than that of in the DDC, though in comparison to UDC, they are less. In the prescribed sequence of categories time comes last, being the most abstract of all the categories (certainly we cannot catch it nor touch it!). In the facet formula it is represented as [T] and in the class number it is indicated by an inverted comma. Here are some examples to illustrate the kind and use of time category.

Travelling in Snow Times
U8‘p8

History of India in 100 BC
V 44‘ C899

Indian Struggle for Freedom (1857 to 1947)
V 44 : 51 ‘N 471 ← M 57

Future of Libraries in India
2.44 ‘P →

Space

In the facet formulà it is indicated as [S]. In the class number it is indicated by a dot, "." In the PMEST sequence it comes after energy. It means that it is less concrete than energy, but more concrete than time. Any division of earth such as physiographical, orientational, political and administrative units, or population clusters are manifestations of the space category. World, Asia, India, Punjab, Amritsar, Middle East countries, South Asia, Eastern Europe, UNO, Arab League, G-8, developing countries, rice growing countries, oil producing countries, Muslim countries, English speaking world, French Empire; hills, mountains, valleys, deserts, forests, seas, rivers all are examples of the space category in the CC. It occurs mostly in social sciences. Following examples will illustrate the space category.

Taxation System in USA
X72.73

Social Security Systems for Workers in UNO countries
X : 958.1N4

Female Education in Muslim countries
T 55.1(Q 7)

Land Transport in Mountains
X 41.g7

Energy

Next to personality, it is the most important facet—as important that from its indicator digit Colon, ":" the scheme draws its name, the Colon Classification. In the facet formula it is represented as [E]. In its order of concreteness it lies halfway of all the five categories. It means it is as concrete as it is abstract. As compared to Space and Time categories energy poses some difficulties in identification or detection. There seems no single term which may comprehensively define the category energy as it exists under various main classes. However, broadly we can say that it is the manifestation of action, reaction, problem, solution. process and operation. Linguistically speaking, verb takes the form of energy in the CC.

In Library Science, energy manifests itself in the technical processing of documents and other library operations; in Mathematics, it is solution to theorems; in Chemistry it is the chemical manipulation, and in Technology it is the industrial process. In Life Sciences, energy wears the vesture of morphology, anatomy, physiology, diseases, their diagnosis.

cure and prevention. In Linguistics, it is the philological problem such as grammar, phonetics and composition. In Psychology it takes the form of cognitive process, feelings, personality. In Education it is characterised by curriculum, teaching technique, measuring students ability, and educational management. In political science and History it is function, power and policy of the state. In Economics, it is trade, transport, consumption, production, management and labour problems. In Sociology energy takes the form of social institutions, civilization, culture, social pathology and welfare:

Cataloguing
2 : 55

Sound Velocity
C5 : 21

Analytical Chemistry
E : 3

Aves Physiology
K96 : 3

Human diseases
L : 4

Pronunciation of English words
P111, 3 : 1

Christian Scriptures
Q 6 : 2

Educational Curriculum
T : 2

Functions of a President
W , 1 : 2

Production (Economics)
X : 2

Social Pathology
Y : 4

Matter

As the name suggests it is the material facet, something less concrete than Personality but more concrete than Energy, Space and Time. It lends itself as a medium to be acted upon (kind of surface in Paintings: material in sculpture): or a commodity for consumption (wine in metabolism). It is something passive on which energy facet acts. For example, in Library Science matter is the kind of document, whether books, periodicals, manuscripts or microforms or an CD. In physiology, it is substance which goes into the body; in nitrogen metabolism, nitrogen is the matter—something being consumed. In Textile it is the thread material. In Music it is the kind of musical instrument. In money (Economics) it is the paper or the kind of metal—the medium of currency. In the facet formula it is represented as [M], and in the class number it is indicated by a semicolon ";"

Microfilms in a Library
2 ; 1512
Gold currency
X61 ; 1
Paintings on Ivory Surface
NQ ; 8
Sulphur Metabolism
G : 33 ; 161

In most of the subjects this category remains absent.

Personality

Of all the five categories, Personality is the most concrete and most difficult to recognize. Like human personality it is an elusive something. It imparts a distinct personality to the subject. It bestows an identity upon the subject. Without it a subject may be formless—without a visage. Let us consider the subjects:

1. Atomic Weight
2. Atomic Weight of sulphur
3. Constitution
4. Indian Constitution

The subjects 2 and 4 are more distinct and identity holders than the subjects 1 and 3 respectively. Personality incarnates itself in persons (individual or groups), institutions, substances, chemicals, kind of life or plant, body organs, languages, religions and the like. In Library Science, the various kinds of libraries constitute the personality; in Chemistry the chemical substance; in life sciences the kind of life; in Agriculture, the agricultural produce; in Medicine the body organ; and in Fine Arts, the style (what else can give personality to an art) constitute personality. Language is the personality in linguistics and literature. In Psychology and education individuals form the personality; while in sociology, history and law, human groups constitute personality.

Since the personality facet in a subject is difficult to be recognized, therefore, Ranganathan has prescribed the **Residual Method** for its identification. A simple logic works here. It consists in eliminating one by one all the other easily recognizable categories, starting from the identification of Time Facet. Since the number of categories never exceeds five, so if the other four categories have been identified, then obviously the remainder one will be the Personality. Chemists usually employ this method in salt analysis.

To illustrate, let us take a title "Cataloguing of Periodicals in University Libraries". In this subject, whose main class is 2 Library Science, we can see at the outset that the time and space categories are absent. Energy is cataloguing and the periodical (being the kind of document) is the matter facet. Now what is left in the residue, i.e., University library, must be the personality. In the facet formula, it is represented as [P] and in the class numbers it is indicated by a comma ",". There are also cases where personality facet does not require any indicator digit. **When personality immediately follows a main or canonical class, then no comma is put, nor it is usually put between [P3] and [P4], [E] and [2P].**

University Libraries
234

Invertebrate Zoology
K 1

Human Eyes
L 185

Pox Disease
L : 423

Here in 423 [E] and [2P] are combined

Child Psychology
S1

Female Education
T55

Indian History
V44

Hindu Law
Z (Q2)

US Law
Z73

Synthesis

After analysis, the next stage is of synthesis. Synthesis is the process of fitting the identified categories in the facet formula. The general facet formula is the same in every case. The absent categories are not mentioned in the formula. This has become possible since the 4th edition (1952) of the CC when the rigidity of the facet formula was done away with. Though every main class has its own facet formula, yet the general formula is the same in every case.

It seems that apparently the intellectual work, rather almost the essence of classifying must end with the analysis into categories. This is not so. Had this been so, there would have been no need at all of giving so many pages of rules or instructions for the synthesis of class numbers. The entire Part I of the sixth edition of the CC consists exclusively of the rules for synthesis and also gives peculiar rules applicable exclusively to a particular main class. It seems, in the CC there are more exceptions than the rules; and the CC abounds with such rules special to each main class. Therefore, the rules are quite essential. Rules supplement the schedules. Rules are not conservative: they are creative, as many more facets can be formed with the help of rules, in some main classes, for which no indication at all has been given in the schedule. It has convincingly been suggested by A.C. Foskett that instead of giving in a separate part it would be better to place the schedule and the correspondingly rules interleaved together side by side.[7] This has been done in the CC-7 (1987).

Apart from the special rules, it is necessary to master some more concepts, such as those of Rounds and Levels, Systems and Specials; and Phase relation—the latter being a device to classify mostly inter-disciplinary subjects. Also important is the method of attaching common isolates. One should also be familiar with the situations where one category masquerades or officiates as other category—Space and Time often officiate as personality in some cases. Devices are also used to make some existing isolates more specific and precise to handle unexpected or local situations. Devices can also be used to create altogether a new isolate, if it does not exist already.

Rounds and Levels

In a subject, a category may exhibit itself in more than one facet. Though Ranganathan fixed the upper limit of the number of categories to five only, but it is not uncommon for the number of facets to be more than five in a class number—even if one or two categories are absent. In the main class Literature we usually experience that only category present is personality, but the number of facets there are four, viz. Language, Form, Author and Work. This phenomenon is explainable through his postulate of Rounds and Levels. In the creation of Rounds and Levels many people feel the backdoor admittance of more number of categories on Ranganathan's part.

In the facet formula the first set of Personality, Matter and Energy forms the first Round. But these categories may also recur: whenever the category Energy recurs it starts a new Round. And within any Round whether first, second or third, Personality and Matter may recur. Recurrence of Personality, Matter, Space and Time within the same round is termed as Levels. Since, to repeat again, whenever Energy facet comes again it starts a new Round, so Energy has no levels but Rounds. Space and Time come only in the last, so they have no Round but Levels only.

In the generalized skeleton facet formula, Round number is indicated by prefixing that number to the facet, while a Level number of a facet is indicated by suffixing that number to facet. For example:

[2E] means Second Round Energy
[P_2] means Second Level Personality
[2P] means Second Round Personality
[$2P_2$] means Second Round Second Level Personality
[3M] means Third Round Matter

Usually for the first Round or Level no number is affixed or suffixed. This convention seems to have been borrowed from the algebra. Hence,

[2P] means Second Round First Level Personality
[P_2] means First Round Second Level Personality, and similarly,
[P_4] means First Round Fourth Level Personality.

But lately this universal convention is being discarded and now usually the first Round or Level is indicated by prefixing or suffixing 1, as the case may be. Now First Round Second Level Personality is indicated as [$1P_2$] and Second Round First Level Personality is indicated as [$2P_1$]. Similarly [$3M_1$] means Third Round First Level Matter.

The general formula is :

(MC), [$1P_1$], [$1P_2$].., [$1P_n$] ; [$1M_1$] : [$1M_2$]...; [$1M_n$]
: [E], [$2P_1$], [$2P_2$],...., [$2P_n$] ; [$2M_1$] ;
[$2M_2$] ; [$2M_3$]...........; [$2M_n$]
: [2E], [$3P_1$].........
....
: [n-1E], [nP_1], [nP_2]...; [nM_1] ;
[nM_n]. [S_1]. [S_2] '[T_1] '[T_2]

Some examples will clarify the concept of Rounds and Levels.

Eyes of Birds

In this subject, which falls in the main class Zoology, both the Birds, and Eyes fall in the Personality category. Here Birds and Eyes constitute the first and second levels respectively:

(Zoology) [Birds], [Eyes]
K96, 185

Phosphorus Metabolism in Animal Bones
K, [bones] : [Metabolism] : [Phosphorus]
K, 82 : 33 ; 151

Here Bone is [1P_2] and Phosphorus is [2M_1] as the latter occurs after [1E].

Treatment of Human Diseases
L : [Disease] : [Treatment]

Here Diseases and Treatment both are Energy facets
L : 4 : 6

In Literature, the Personality occurs four Times :
O [P1], [P_2] [P_3], [P_4]
O [Language], [Form] [Author], [Work]

Shakespeare's Hamlet
O 111, 2J64, 51

In this class number there are four levels of Personality.

Teaching of Mathematics
Education : [Teaching] [Mathematics]
T : 3 (B)

Here Mathematics is [2P_1].

Theoretically there is no limit to the Rounds of Energy and the Levels which may occur within any round—as it is clear from the generalized skeleton formula. Practically from the schedule of sixth edition of the scheme, we see that at the most Energy occurs twice. It means that there are three Rounds only. The main classes, where Energy occurs twice are J Agriculture, KZ, Animal Husbandry, L Medicine. S Psychology and Y Sociology.

Only in C Physics and all the Life Sciences matter occurs as [2M]. Ranganathan at rule 0564, page 1.27 of CC (1963) also gives one example of L Medicine where matter occurs as [3M]. Matter may occur in first, second or third round, but nowhere it exhibits any level other than the first, empirically speaking.

Speaking similarly of the Personality, we see that in extreme cases the Personality occurs in three Rounds. Cases where Personality occurs in three rounds are the same where Energy occurs twice viz., the main classes, J, KZ, L, S and Y. In the first Round, Personality may occur in four levels in extreme in the case of a Generalia Bibliography. N Fine Arts, O Literature and Z Law. In B33 Differential and Integral Equations and P Linguistics, Personality occurs in three levels. And the cases where Personality occurs in two levels in first round are quite numerous—in the main classes B, D, E, F, G, HZ, I, K, KZ, L, R, V, and W. Of the occurrence of [2P], we see that it is hand and glove with [E], so it occurs in almost all the schedules, O and U are exceptions, however. [$2P_2$] occurs only in E : 3 Analytical Chemistry and T Education.

Space and Time may both occur in two levels. But only in the last round—they have no round.

It may be noticed that throughout the schedules (with only one or two exceptions) the problem facet is marked as "[E] cum [2P]". It means all the isolates under such levels present [E] and [2P] combined, not separately. C.D. Batty explains that "It means that some of the activities of the energy facet involve substance or tool which by definition belong to personality facet. Such substances cannot be separated from their associated energy facet activities, so they are called the second round of Personality facet."[8]

Facet Sequence

It may be mentioned that the sequence of facets within a facet formula is not arbitrary. Nor the classifier has to determine every time to which round and to which level of a given round a particular facet will go. It has already been done by the classificationist himself. The classifier need not bother about it, though a simple logic works. Ranganathan has objectified his rationale in fixing the sequence of facets and has capsulated them in his following principles[9]:

1. Wall-Picture Principle
2. Whole-Organ Principle
3. Cow-Calf Principle
4. Act and-Action-Actor-Tool Principle.
5. Commodity Raw Material Principle.

It may be noted that the sequence of facets is a part of the higher principle of **Helpful sequence**. Actually, there can be no absolute helpful sequence which is universal and helpful to all the readers. Needs of readers are individual, therefore, at times the so called Helpful Sequence obtained by the CC may not serve the purpose in a particular situation. Helpful sequence means helpful to most of the readers, not to all. The shelf order of CC may not be helpful to the readers interested in say Area studies or Period studies. We cannot change the order of facets, so as to bring all the books of a particular area together; or to converge at a point all the books about all the subjects pertaining to a given say Renaissance studies or Eighteenth century studies. The UDC has an advantage over the CC, as there the sequence of auxiliaries can be altered. If we wish to place all the subjects relating to India together, so the class numbers, may be altered as:

(540) 33 Indian Economy
(540) 301 Sociology of India
(540) 32 Politics of India

thus forming a separate library on Indology.

Absent, Diffused and Latent Facets

It is not essential for all the categories to be present in a given or all the subjects. It depends upon the depth of the subject, whether it contains facets belonging to all the categories or some are absent. For example, in the title "Classification in the University Libraries", Matter, Space and Time categories are absent. In the title "Atomic Weight", only Energy is present; and in the title "Hindu Religion" only Personality is present and all other categories are absent. In brief it means that any category may be absent, and any category may present itself more than once in a subject. Space and Time coming in the last round may present or absent themselves without much affecting the facet formula. Both of them are usually absent in scientific subjects. However, no Main Class is without a Personality facet, though a given title may be. Matter facet usually remains absent in many main classes—Library Science. Fine Art, Economics and all the Life Sciences are exception, where Matter is present.

Energy though deemed to be an important category is absent in a Generalia Bibliography, U Geography and O Literature. In the rest of the main classes it is present, but in a particular title it may be absent.

Diffused Facet

A facet or category may be omnipresent, but still not present overtly. It may not be crystallized. Its focus is not sharp or pin pointed. It is spread all over the facet. Such a facet is a diffused facet. For example, in the title "classification in libraries", which belongs to the main class Library Science wherein kinds of libraries make the Personality. In the title in question, since no particular kind of library has been mentioned, so it is true for all the Personality facets. Hence the Personality is diffused. In synthesis it is treated like an absent facet. The class number for the subject thus is 2 : 51. "Human Diseases" is another example where Personality is diffused. Let us take another example "Social Evils". Sociology is a study of social groups. Since in the above title no particular group has been mentioned, so it belongs to all but is specific to none. Hence it is diffused. Diffused facet in effect is an absent facet.

Latent Facet

Presence of a facet in a subject may be only implied or suggestive. In a Raw title, a facet may be hidden. For example, in the title "wheat storage", storage is a secondary operation. It cannot take place before harvesting has been done. So the facet "Harvesting" is a hidden or latent facet. Before assigning the class number, the hidden facet must be improvised at its proper place in the facet sequence. It is a prerequisite :

[Agriculture] [Wheat] : [Harvesting] : [Storage]
J 382 : 7 : 8

Usually the latent facet is [1E] when in the subject both the [1E] and [2E] are present. It means that the concept behind the [2E] cannot be realized unless [E] already exists. But it is not true with all the facets:

[2P] may occur irrespective of the presence or absence of [P]. [2M] or even [3M] occur without the prior existence of [M] or [2M], as the case may be. Similarly a level of [P], [S] or [T] may occur without any conditional existence of their earlier levels: [P_1] is not a necessity for the occurrence of [P_2] or higher levels.

Steps of Practical Classification

When all the categories have been identified and the latent facets have been supplied, they are arranged in the facet formula given for each subject—the facet formula is a general one. Next step is to standardise the terms. In the facet formula the standard terms are replaced by their isolate numbers preceded by their respective indicator digits. All these steps have been explained in a graded fashion by Ranganathan. These are steps for practical classification which is a slow and dull method for classifying. But the practice gained through this approach makes a user an impeccable classifier. Once you become adept in classifying, this approach is no more required. An experienced classifier either bypasses or mentally observes the steps required in practical classification. This approach has been explained in Sec. 0261 (pages 1.7 to 1.8) of the Rule portion of CC and in other various books of Ranganathan.

REFERENCES

1. Though most of the main classes are traditional, but their boundaries always remain changing. New main classes emerge either from the inter-disciplinary action of two or more subjects (Geopolitics), or from the fission of a given subject (statistics from mathematics). Ranganathan very well knew this tendency and accordingly provided devices to interpolate the new (MC)s.
2. For a diagram of this pattern see author's *An Epistle to Dean Shera on the Brevity of Notation in Colon Classification*, Amritsar, Rajat. 1979, p. 22.
3. This is postulated by CC Rule 12, page 1.42.
4. *Prolegomena* Ed. 3, Sec JC 1, p. 266.
5. Rule 12 page 1.42 CC ed. 6.
6. CC Rule 05121 page 1.22.
7. A.C. Foskett, *The Subject Approach to Information*, 2nd ed. London, Clive Bingley, 1971, p. 274.
8. C.D. Batty, *Introduction to Colon Classification*, London, Clive Bingley, 1967, p. 37.
9. Explained in Ranganathan, S.R. *Prolegomena*, ed. 3, Bombay, Asia, Chaps RM and RN, pp. 425-28.

2

COMMON SCHEDULES

An isolate is smallest and indivisible unit of knowledge. Isolates are of two kinds : Common Isolates and Special Isolates. Common Isolates, which are applicable to every main class and its class number, are the manifestations of the mode of expression, viewpoint or the physical media of documents. These are not subject divisions. Since these remain the same for every subject, so their schedule has been given once for all on pages 2.5-2.6. But the special isolates are different and unique for every subject. Hence the name special isolates. Isolates under all the Five Fundamental Categories are special isolates. But the isolates belonging to the categories of Space and Time remain as such whatever be the subject. They do not change from subject to subject. Therefore, the isolates of these two categories remain the same. Same is the case with the Language isolates. Their names and Isolates numbers are the same both under the main classes O Literature and P Linguistics. These can also be used as such in the Book Numbers. Hence the name common schedules. In such schedules isolates are used as they are enumerated, while in some cases the isolates for these schedules have to be sharpened or constructed anew by the use of the devices.

Schedules of Space Isolates, Time Isolates and Language Isolates are applicable as such wherever required. Therefore, they have been enumerated once for all. In such schedules many isolates are used as they are enumerated, while in other cases the isolates have to be constructed by the use of the devices.

A. Space Isolates

It is a common facet attachable wherever warranted. Its indicator digit is inverted comma. Its isolates have been enumerated in Chapter 4 of the schedules (pp. 2.8-2.17 and p. 26 of the Annexure). Rules for applying them and constructing or sharpening Space Isolates (wherever necessary) have been given in Chapter 4 of the Rules (pp. 1.51-1.53 and pp. 20-23 of the Annexure).

Space Isolates occur at two levels [S_1] and [S_2]. Isolates in [S_1] are denoted by numerical digits (of course decimal in character); whereas [S_2] isolates are denoted by small alphabets and numerical digits, if necessary. First Level division of the earth is Political (Asia, India, Punjab), Zonal (equitorial, tropical), Directional (East, South-East, West) and population and administrative units (village, town, or city).

The digit 1 stands for the world as a whole, which has further been divided by zones and orientation. The digit 2 stands for the Mother country and 3 for the Favoured country. The digits 4 to 8 represent the various continents which have further been divided into countries. The last digit 9 represents the various islands and the oceans. But apart from these enumerated isolates many more can be constructed by (SD) (Muslim countries, for example), (CD) (League of Nations, for example) and (SID) (French Empire, for example).

Superimposition Device (SID) is employed to construct an isolate number for an empire having colonies in different and scattered areas of the world. The dominated area comes first and the dominating nation comes later :

British India
44-56

British Colonies in the World
1-56

French Africa
6-53

Colonial America
73-56

Subject Device (SD) is used to represent areas of the world having a common characteristic. For example, Agricultural countries, Under-developed countries, Oil Producing countries, Christian countries, English Speaking countries, European monarchies. This is done usually by sharpening the appropriate area by the (SD) :

English speaking countries (of the world)
1(P111)

English speaking countries of Europe
5(P111)

Catholic Europe
5(Q62)

European Monarchies
5(W4)

Rice Growing States of India
44(J381)

Communist Countries
1(W691)

(SID) and (SD) may also be used in succession, if need arises, though in the schedule there are no specific instructions for this :

Rice Growing States in British India
44-56 (J 381)

Sparsely populated areas of French Africa
6-53 (Y : 581)

Chronological Device (CD) is employed to get the isolate number for near sovereign international organizations. This is done by sharpening the appropriate area by (CD) :

League of Nations
1N

SAARC
4N8

CENTO Central Treaty Organization (1967)
1N67

Council of Europe (1949)
5N49

Association of South East Asian Nations (ASEAN) Countries
43N67

Organization of African Unity (OAU 1963)
6N6

Organization of American States (1948)
7N48

(CD) and (SD) may also be used together :

Communist Member Countries of UNO
1N4(W 691)

Similarly,

European Members of the UNO
1N4-5

The isolate number for population clusters such as city Tehsil, Village, if not enumerated is got by Alphabetical Device (AD). The method of applying (AD) here is a bit different. A dot "." is put between the appropriate upper area and (AD), (Rule 4B Annexure)

Punjab	4443
Amritsar city	4443.A
Ludhiana	4443.L
Chennai city	4411.C

Paris	53.P
Zurich	594.Z

Any geographical area may further be subdivided by orientation as the division of 1 world, by orientation divisions given from 19A to 19Y. It means that an orientation division is attached to any area with a dot "." and Orientation number after deleting the initial digit 1

Eastern Europe
5.9 B

Central Punjab
4443.9 D

East of Amritsar
4443.A. 9 B

If the orientation division of any area is given by enumeration, then it must not be got by synthesis. For example, since North America is enumerated as 71, so to get its number by synthesis as 7.9S is wrong. Similarly, South East Asia is 43 enumerated, so to make its number as 4.9F is wrong.

Isolate number for a greater Metropolitan city is to be got **not** from the division of the state to which it belongs, but by the division of the country itself :

Bombay
44.B

Inside of Bombay
44.B.9 X

Calcutta
44.C

West Calcutta
44.C.9M

One more important point to be noted is that for India, two schedules for Space Isolates have been provided. Now it is better to use the schedule marked as "After 1956". It begins at First column of the page 2.12.

The Second Level [S_2] representing physical features of the earth obviously comes after the First Level; and its isolates have been enumerated at page 26 of the Annexure. The indicator digit for [S_2] is also the dot ".".

Rainfall in Forests
U 2855.f

Sea Travels
U8.r

Fauna and Flora of Forests
G : 12.f

Fauna and Flora of Indian Forests
G : 12.44.f

[S_2] may be sharpened by (AD) in case of specifically named physical features. But here [S_1] should be as broad as possible.

Plants of Gangetic Valley
I : 13.44.g1G

Travels in Himalayan Mountains
U8.4.g7H

Weather forecasting in Nilgiri Hills
U2891.44.g7N

Gobi Desert-Geography
U. 41.dG

Nile River-Geography
U.6.p1N

Here [S_2] p1 River has been sharpened by (AD) N standing for Nile river.

Space Isolates impersonate as Personality Isolates in canonical classes NA to NR, V History and Z Law, and also in Common Isolates. Whenever a Geographical Isolate officiates as personality, its indicator digit must be changed to comma from dot. For example :

History of Madras City
V4411, M

Amritsar in 1939
V4443, A' N39

B. Time

Isolates for the Time facet have been enumerated in chapter 3 of the Schedule (page 2.7). The rules for using and constructing them (if necessary) have been given in chapter 3 of the Rules (pages 1.49-1.50). Time facet occurs in two levels. [T_1] is the chronological Time period and [T_2] is the cyclical Time known as featured Time.

[T_1] is denoted by Roman capital alphabets followed by Indo-Arabic digits. The first digit A stands for Geological Times. With the other digits from B to YC we can represent any particular year or a span of time falling between 9999 BC to 3199 AD. This period has not been distributed averagely among the available digits, but by the principle of proportionate allocation of digits. This method secures brevity in notation for the oft used isolate numbers.

A	:	Denotes Geological Ages
B-C	:	Denote Before Christ (BC) era
B	:	Represents the period from 9999BC to 1000BC; and
C	:	Encompasses the time from 999BC to 1BC. From the digit D onwards starts the present era, viz., A.D. era.
D	:	Represents the first thousand years, i.e., 1 to 999 AD, while from E onwards each digit represents a century :
E	:	Stands for the Eleventh Century;
		....
K	:	Denotes the Seventeenth, while the twentieth century has been denoted by the digit N, 21st century by P and so on.

The CC can measure Time only upto a particular year, not up to the particular month or day as the UDC can. From the digits E to YC each year is represented by three digits. The first digit (the alphabetical letter) represents the century, the first numerical digit (or the second digit in general) denotes the decade and the last digit the year particular. For example :

1526 A.D. is denoted as J 26
J stands for the 16th century

J 2 stands for the 3rd decade of the 16th century and J 26 stands for 1526, the exact year. Similarly, the year 1901 AD is indicated as N 01 and 2002 as P 02; the year 1800 AD as M00, and 1850 as M50. The 1880's are represented as M8. Nineteen-twenties (1920s) are denoted as N2, very obviously.

But in case of D, any year belonging to the first millennium AD is indicated by four digits in total—one alphabet and three numerical digits. The first digit denotes the millennium, the second digit, (the first numerical digit) the century, third the decade, and fourth the year exact. 212AD is indicated as D212. 5AD is denoted as D005 and 110AD is denoted as D110 and 10AD is denoted as D010 and so on. The sixth century is indicated as D5 and the Tenth by D9. Similarly we can denote any decade falling between these centuries. D65 represents the sixth decade of the seventh century AD, i.e., 650s AD.

BC Time Era

But the BC time cannot be denoted as easily. Complication arises out of the fact that we measure BC time from the opposite direction it flows.

To arrange books in the increasing chronological order, Ranganathan devised, what he calls the **Method of Complements**. This method consists in subtracting the year to be denoted from the higher numerical limit (actually the lowest point) denoted by that digit. Say, we wish to denote 1200 BC. The period of 1200 BC is covered by the span represented by the digit B. The highest limit, (actually the lowest) represented by B is 9999 BC, so to denote 1200 BC, it must be subtracted from 9999. Thus 1200 BC is denoted as (9999-1200) B8799. Similarly 5000 BC is denoted as B4999; 6000BC is denoted as B3999, and so on. Similarly 999 BC is indicated as C000, 10 BC is indicated as C989 and 5 BC is indicated as C994.

Though B8799 does not reveal as easily that it denotes 1200 BC as easily J64 reveals that it is 1564 AD. But this is the only simple[1] method to maintain the strict chronological order.

Effective Decade: In many a case, especially in social sciences, the indication of the exact year of time is meaningless and unnecessary. Decade is an arbitrary division, convenient only for calculations. There is nothing intrinsically social in it. The effective unit to measure social change seems to be a generation—which consists of two decades. Ranganathan terms a period of two decades as an **Effective Decade**. He postulates that the 2nd, 4th, 6th, 8th and 10th decades denoted by the digit 1, 3, 5, 7 and 9 respectively are the **Effective Decade Numbers**. To clarify further, a table is given below on the use of Effective Decade :

Actual Decades Digits	*Span of Years of the Century*	*Effective Decade Digit*
0 or 1	0-19	1
2 or 3	20-39	3
4 or 5	40-59	5
6 or 7	60-79	7
8 or 9	80-99	9

To illustrate, Effective Decade for the year 1981 is N9; the (ED) for 1900 AD is N1; and for 1859 it is M5; and for 1841 it is also M5. The above table will help. There are many cases where the rules in the CC prescribe the use of (ED). This has been discussed under the Chronological device (CD). The Latest Effect decade is denoted as (LED) accordingly.

Second Level Time Facet: [T_2] stands for the seasonal, meteorological or diurnal times. The indicator digit for [T_2] is the same as that of [T_1]—inverted comma :

Cow Feeding in Winter
KZ 311 : 1 'n7

Human Migration in Snow Times
U42 'p8

Humidity in Rainy Season of 1995
U285 'N95 'p5

[T_2] is mostly used in U Geography.

In case of Paleontology, Paleobotany or Paleozoology, Time is not to be taken from the chapter 3, but from the canonical class H5 Stratigraphy. In this case H5 is to be replaced by A. In the schedule of Time Isolates (Chapter 3, p. 2.7) the digit A stands for Geological periods and it has been seen that no contradiction arises by this method. The isolates thus got come as the extension of the digit A of the Time Schedule.

Silurian Paleozoology
H6 'A23

(Here silurian is H523, since H5 is to be replaced by A, so H523 = A23)

Similarly Cainozoic Plants
I : 8 'A4

The cases where Time Isolates function as Personality have been discussed under the heading Chronological Device (CD) given elsewhere.

IT MAY BE NOTED THAT THROUGHOUT THE SCHEDULES THE TIME FACET HAS BEEN INDICATED BY A DOT. SINCE 1963, THE INDICATOR DIGIT FOR TIME FACET HAS BEEN CHANGED TO SINGLE INVERTED COMMA. THEREFORE, THROUGHOUT THE RULES AND SCHEDULES OF THE CC THE DOT SHOULD BE REPLACED BY AN INVERTED COMMA IN CASE OF TIME FACET.*

C. Language Schedule

A particular language forms the personality facet in O Literature and P Linguistics : and Language Isolates are also used in the Book Number. Therefore, Ranganathan has enumerated them once for all in chapter 5 of the schedules (pages 2.26-2.27). Some of the major families of languages have been enumerated from isolate numbers 1 to 3. Enumeration of individual members of these families is fairly detailed. But the enumeration is limited to the languages most known and spoken by a large number of population. In enumeration, not only many individual languages have been omitted, but many families of languages have been altogether omitted without a trace. There are, of course, some rules to provide isolate numbers to such unenumerated languages.

* See CC-6 (1963), p. 19 (Annexure).

1. Indo-European Languages
2. Semitic Languages
3. Dravidian Languages

4-9 Other Languages to be got by (GD)

99 Artificial Languages to be got by (CD)

If a language definitely belongs to any family denoted by 1, 2 or 3 or their sub-divisions, but not enumerated there, may be got by adding 9 to the approximate language number and it should be further sharpened by the (GD).

For example, Rumanian Language has not been enumerated in the schedule. It belongs to the sub-family of Latin Languages. Thus its isolate number may be got as:

12+9+5921 Area number of Rumania = 1295921

Similarly

Bihari (it belongs to the Sankrit sub-family)
15+9+4473 = 1594473

Baluchi (it belongs to Iranian sub-family)
16944Q75

Czech
1495925

Serbo-Croatian
149523

Breton
128923

Yiddish (Teutonic language spoken by Jews)
1194653

Afrikaans (Teutonic sub-family)
11963

Maltese (Semitic sub-family spoken in Malta)
295292

Coptic (Semitic sub-family spoken in Egypt)
29677

Languages not belonging to the above families are got by (GD).

Japanese Language
42

Korean Language
495

Australian (aboriginal)
8

Sibo (Spoken in North Western China)
41

Nakhi (Spoken in Yunnan Province of Southern China)
4141

Burmese
438

Thai
433

Malay
435

Indonesian Language
436

Delaware
7314

Fijian
9368

Burmese Language (it belongs to Sino-Tibetan family). Since this family has not been enumerated, so it is got by (GD).
438

Hungarian
5932

Khmer (National Language of Cambodia)
4315

Hungarian
5932

Quite a good number of isolates for artificial languages have been enumerated; others may be got by (CD) :

Occidental (1922)
99N2

Novial (1928)
99N28

International Picture Language (1931)
99N3

Interglossa
99N4

All the languages have different stages caused by time, and variations caused by distance. The latter phenomena is known as dialects of languages. Ranganathan has provided elaborated rules to provide numbers for stages or dialects of any language. These have been discussed in the chapter on P Linguistics.

REFERENCE

1. The other method could be to denote the BC era as a negative time, as does the UDC. But that could give way to a notational crisis. Firstly because in the CC all the numerical digits have positive value; so denoting BC time as a negative time could complicate the matter. Secondly the minus sign and the hyphen, the latter being already used in the CC, resemble each other quite. If both were used, it would be very hard to distinguish between these two so closely resembling notational symbols. Therefore, the present method of complements is an ingenious device to keep the documents in an increasing chronological sequence.

3

COMMON ISOLATES

An isolate in the CC is a fundamental and ultimate unit of knowledge. By itself it cannot stand; so alone it cannot make a subject. Isolates enumerated specially and exclusively for a particular main class are termed **Special Isolates**. In contrast to these, isolates enumerated once for all and which remain the same for every main class are veritably termed as **Common Isolates**.

It may be stated that the Common Isolates (CI) are mere auxiliaries, and not part of the subject proper. They are recurring concepts and mostly pertain to the form of presentation taking into view the extra-textual considerations. Since they are listed once for all, their names and notational symbols remain the same wherever they occur. The DDC aptly called them Form Divisions and now more appropriately as the Standard Sub-divisions as they have been renamed lately. Of the common isolates Ranganathan maintains that they are attachable to most of the classes, *though not all*. They stand for divisions such as encyclopaedia, dictionary, periodical, bibliography, statistics or forms of presentation such as history, commission report and conference proceedings. Institutions, research, criticism, are also Common Isolates.

To arrange the subjects in a real Apupa pattern much depends upon these Common Isolates. These form divisions impart shades of various intensity to the core of a subject. Rather, without Common Isolates there can be no Apupa pattern. Not only this, with even one kind of Common Isolates, as in the case of DDC, there cannot be the real Apupa pattern.

Ranganathan divided the Common Isolates into two categories and further sub-categories, which may be best represented diagrammatically as on page 50.

Broadly speaking they are of two kinds :

(1) Anteriorising Common Isolates (ACI)
(2) Posteriorising Common Isolates (PCI)

(ACI) : When attached to a subject they give it an anterior position over other subjects of the same class. Their another feature is that they do not require any connecting symbol. Documents attached with anteriorising Common Isolates form the approach documents on the shelves. They are of three kinds.

A. (ACI)s Attachable Before Space

Dictionary of Library Science
2k
Dictionary of Library Classification
2 : 51k
Dictionary of Colon Classification
2 : 51N3k

2k, 2 : 51k and 2 : 51N3k will file before 2, 2 : 51 and 2 : 51N3 respectively (Rule 0251 page 1.6). (ACI)s have their own facet formula fitted with first and second levels of Personality:

Class number ACI $[P_1]$, $[P_2]$

The symbols for the (ACI)s and their facet formula have been given at pages 2.5 and 2.6 of the schedules, while the rules for applying them have been given on pages 1.43 to 1.47.

Generally $[P_1]$ is the area of purview or the locality of origin to be got by (GD). $[P_2]$ is the epoch of origin to be got by (CD). While applying (CD) only the minimum digits are required for individualizing. But in the (ACI) formula, if there is only first level of personality then it is to be got by (CD), instead of (GD).

Bibliography on Shakespeare brought upto 1981
O111, 2J64aN9
Geographical Atlas (1970)
UfN7
(Here [T] is to be got by the (LED)
Herald of Library Science, India, 1962+)
2m44, N62
IASLIC Bulletin
IASLIC Newsletter

(Let us suppose that both of them were started in the year 1957)

Their class number respectively are:

2m44, N57
2m44, N 57, 1
(Rule 21m3, page 1.46)

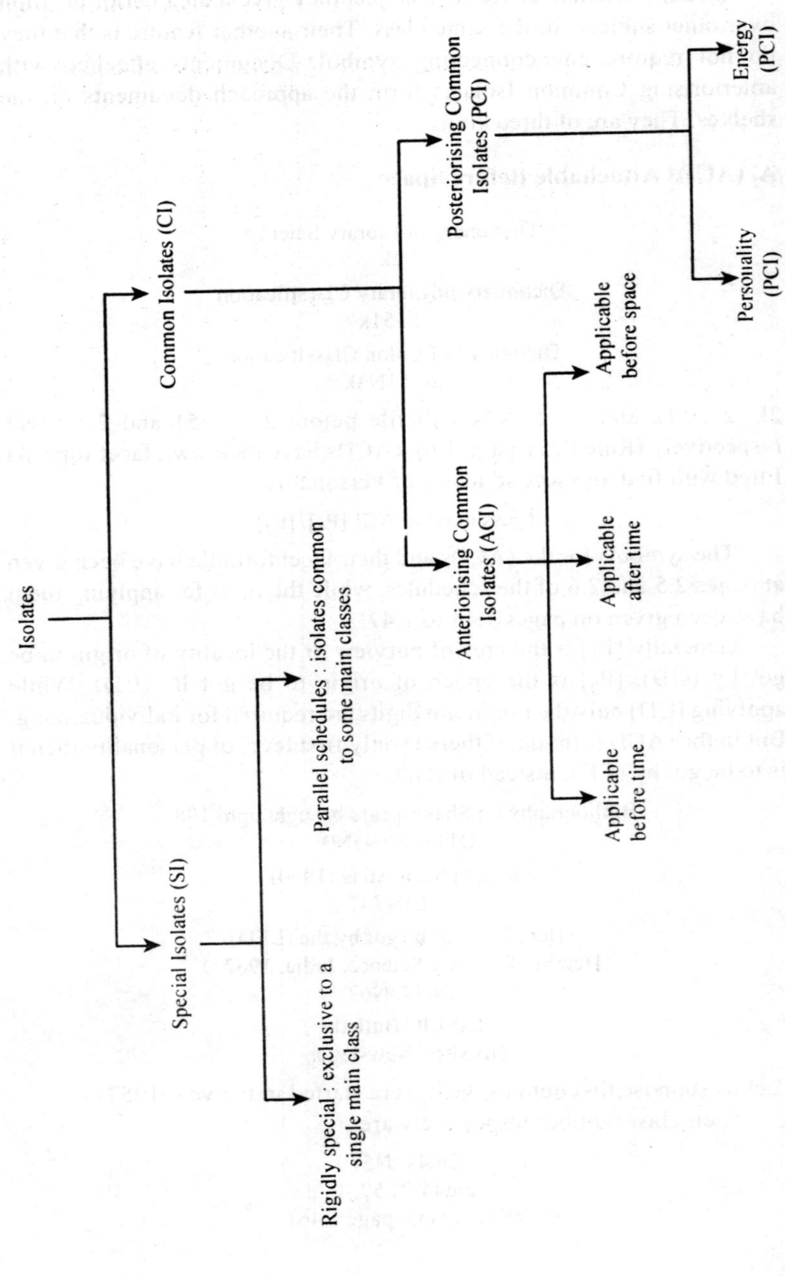
Isolates
Common Isolates (CI)
Special Isolates (SI)
Posteriorising Common Isolates (PCI)
Anteriorising Common Isolates (ACI)
Energy (PCI)
Personality (PCI)
Applicable before space
Applicable after time
Applicable before time
Parallel schedules : isolates common to some main classes
Rigidly special : exclusive to a single main class

History of Indian Librarianship brought upto 1990's
2v44 'N9

In case of w biography, w is to be fitted with [T], to be got by the exact year of birth in case of an individual's biography, and with (LED) covered in case of collective biographies.

Biography of Ranganathan (birth 1892)
2wM92

Life of Charles Darwin (birth 1809)
GwM09

In case the biographer happens to be a protagonist, rather than a theoretical writer, the w is to be replaced by y7.

Life of Nehru
V44y7 M89

Life of Hitler
V55y7M92

Life of Harold Laski
WwM52

Life of Eva Braun (Mistress of Hitler)
V55y7M92

(She will get the class number for the biography of Hitler. It is presumed that someone will be interested in her life only for the sake of Hitler, so both the biographies will get the same class number).

If the Time Facet is already included in the class number, it may not be repeated. It will happen usually in case of O Literature:

Life of John Keats (birth 1792)
O111, 1L92w

Biography of Shakespeare
O111, 2J64w

Similarly in case of collected works :

Collected works of Ranganathan
2xM92

Collected works of Melvil Dewey
2xM51

Biographies of Indian Biologists (youngest born in 1939)
Gw44, N3

Works of British Mathematicians (youngest born in 1945)
Bx56, N5

B. Applicable After Space Facet

Indian Economic Tables started in 1970
X.44sN

(Only minimum digits are to be used for individualizing)

C. Applicable After Time Facet

Report of the Advisory Committee on Libraries (India, 1957)
2.44 'N57t

Indian Labour Statistics for 1950's
X : 9.44 'N5s

Whenever warranted two (ACI)s may be applied in succession:

Library Science Abstracts
2am

Bibliography of Library Science Periodicals brought upto 1970
2maN7

Indian National Biography (Started, say in, 1969)
wn44, N6

Posteriorising Common Isolates (PCI)

As contrasted from the (ACI)s, (PCI)s are quite different. Firstly, they give posterior position to the document to which they are attached. It means a class number fitted with a (PCI) will come after the same class number without it. Secondly they require a connecting symbol for their attachment. They are of two kinds:

(1) Energy (PCI)
(2) Personality (PCI)

(1) Posteriorising Energy Common Isolates are attached with a Colon:

Literary Criticism
O : g

Experiments on the velocity of ultraviolet light
C52 : 21 : f3

Research in Colon Classification
2 : 51N3 : f

Weighing Gases
C 28 : c1

Surveys for Cycle Exports
X 8 (D 5125) : 545 : u

(2) Personality Posteriorising common isolates, attached to any class number with a comma, mostly pertain to institutions and associations. They are enumerated at page 2.6 of the schedules, and the rules for applying them are given at page 1.48. They are applicable after the Space Facet and the formula for them may be put as :

[MC]. [Space], b/w, [P_1], [P_2] : [E]
[MC]. [Space], PCI digit, (AD) or 9 (CD), [P_2] : [E]

Here [P_1] is to be got by (AD) in case of a localised body. But in case of a non-localised body [P_1] is to be got by (CD) but 9 should precede it. **[P_2] and [E] are the same as that of V History**.

Medical Profession in India
L.44, b

Profession of Homeopathy in India
LL.44, b

Institution of Bankers in India (1901)
X 61.44, d, 9 N 01

Functions of the Principal of Khalsa College of Education, Amritsar
T.4443, e4, K, 1 : 3

Here K which is [P_1] has been got by (AD), [P_2] and [E] have been got from the main class V History.

International Council of Scientific Unions (ICSU)
A. 1, g, 9N

Election of the IASLIC President
24.44, g, 9 N 6, 1 : 91

(Here 1 and 91 have been taken from [P_2] and [E] respectively of the (MC) V History)

Association of Commonwealth Universities
T 4. 1N48, g, 9 N5

International Federation of Information and Documentation (FID)
2 : 97.1, d, 9M

It is also possible that a (PCI) and an (ACI) may be applied together in one and the same class number:

Annual Report of the Guru Nanak Dev University, Amritsar
T 4.4443, d, Gr

Report of the Indian Mathematical Society
B.44, g, 9 Nr

Another very curious form of Common Isolates occurs in P Linguistics and Z Law. In [P_3] of P Linguistics the isolate numbers 11 and 15 and their sub-divisions have their own Common Isolates given at page 2.95 (first column). These Common Isolates are applicable there only and nowhere else.

Nasal Consonants
P,1508

Rolled velar consonants of modern English
P 111, J 15303

Similarly in [P_2] 5 of Z Law, 04 Abetment is attachable to all its subdivisions:

Indian Law regarding abetment in breach of contract
Z 44, 5304

Indian Law for abetment of war crimes
Z 44, 5 ZA 04

Some more examples of common isolates are given below:

Collected poetry of Tagore
O157, 1 M 61 x

Hindi short stories (by various authors, (the youngest born in 1940))
O152, 3x N 5

Letters of Charles Darwin
GwM09,4

Letters of Lord Alfred Tennyson
O111, 1 M09,4

Annual Export Statistics of India
X : 545.44s N

Criticism

Common Isolates as devised by Ranganathan help to individualize every document. But Ranganathan is bit presumptuous to think that all the (ACI)s form approach documents to the core subject. Nobody reads periodicals or conference reports before he/she has a sufficient basic knowledge of the subject. Therefore, these should have been placed in a posterior position.

4

DEVICES FOR "SELF-PERPETUATION"

CC class numbers are malleable and ductile. Ranganathan on the dint of his devices meant for sharpening the isolates or to create altogether new ones, always projected his scheme as a self-perpetuating one. It is quite doubtful (or debatable at least) whether any scheme in itself can be self-perpetuating. Nevertheless, these devices equip the scheme to finely individualize those class numbers, which other general enumerative schemes lump *en masse*. With these devices any isolate number can be made quite succinct to suit the occasion. These devices are:

(1)	Chronological Device	(CD)
(2)	Subject Device	(SD)
(3)	Geographical Device	(GD)
(4)	Alphabetical Device	(AD)
(5)	Mnemonic Device	(MD)
(6)	Classic Device	(CD)
(7)	Superimposition Device	(SID)

These devices occupy a dominating place in the armoury of the hospitality devices for the CC. Their nature and use is explained below:

(1) Chronological Device

It is the most widely and easily used device. It is applied where Time is a dominating or inherent factor in the entity. It consists in adding the epoch of origin to the ultimate isolate or class number, whenever necessary or directed. In some cases an isolate may entirely be formed by the (CD).

In the CC all the system facets (SmF) are formed by this device, just by amplifying the (MC), (CC) or the appropriate class number, as the case may be. In case of systems of geometry the canonical class B6 is sharperred by (CD):

B6M Non-Euclidean Geometry
B6M3 Elliptic Geometry
B6N Line Complex Geometry
Religious sects are also got by (CD)
Q68J3 Baptists
Q68L4 New Church
Q68L6 Methodists
Q78M9 Ahamadiya Muslims

System facets in B Mathematics, C Physics, L Medicine, Q Religion, S Psychology, T Education, V History and X Economics, have all been got by (CD).

The places where (CD) is applicable have been indicated. Situations which can be coped with (CD) are very evidently suggestive. From the above examples, it should be clear that it is not necessary that the focus for (CD) should be pinpointed to the exact year. Too much precision may be superfluous and may unnecessarily lengthen the class number. For the sake of simplicity and brevity of notation, Ranganathan prescribes that "for the first isolate in any array, whose epoch falls within a century (or millennium) the first digit alone should be used".[1] He writes further : "among the other isolates calling for the same first digit, the first "isolate whose epoch falls within the same decade (or century) the first two digits should be used".[2] Situations where (CD) is to be got by (ED) or (LED) have also been indicated. This rule aims to achieve individuality in isolate numbers by using minimum number of digits as far as possible. This rule can be best illustrated by the examples of classification schemes:

(1)	Dewey Decimal Classification	(1876)
(2)	Cutter's Expansive Classification	(1891)
(3)	Universal Decimal Classification	(1896)
(4)	Library of Congress Classification	(1904)
(5)	Colon Classification	(1933)
(6)	Bliss' Bibliographic Classification	(1935)

(1)	DDC	2: 51 M	(Being the first scheme of the 19th century)
(2)	EC	2 : 51M9	(Being the second scheme of the 19th century)
(3)	UDC	2 : 51M96	(Being the third scheme of the 19th century : and second of the 10th decade of the 19th century)
(4)	LC	2 : 51N	(Being the first scheme of the 20th century)
(5)	CC	2 : 51N3	(Being the second scheme of the 20th century)
(6)	BC	2 : 51N35	(Being the second scheme of the 4th decade of 20th century)

As said earlier, the other major role of the (CD) is to create an isolate afresh altogether. For example:

[P_2] in NA to NR Fine Arts
[P_3] in O Literature
[P_2] in P Linguistics
[P_2] in (ACI) in many cases

Mughal Paintings
NQ44, J

Author facet in O Literature is always got by the Birth year of a particular author, and in case of anthologies it is got by the (LED) covered:

John Keats
O 111, 1L92

George Bernard Shaw
O 111, 2M56

Prem Chand : Gaudan
O 152, 3M12, G

Anthology of Punjabi poetry
(The youngest author is 1949 born)
O153, 1xN5

In Case of (ACI), [P_2] is got by (CD), subject to the rules 05813 and 05814 (p. 1.29), for the brevity of notation :

Library Journal
2m73, M

Soviet Encyclopaedia
k58, N

American Men of Science
Awn73, N

All India Conference on Colon Classification (1962)
2 : 51N3p44, N62

But in case of collected works, biography, autobiography [P_1] is to be got by (CD)

Collected works of Ranganathan
2x M92

Biography of Ranganathan
2w M92

Also in Personality Posteriorising Common Isolates (PPCI), [P_1] is to be got by (CD), though 9 precedes the (CD)

Indian Library Association
2.44, g, 9N
Indian Association of Information Scientists 1976
2.44,g, 9N76

(2) Subject Device

It is a very potent device which a classifier attempts to employ even at the slightest suggestion. Any part of the class number enclosed between parenthesis is the Subject Device part of the class number. It may be considered analogous to the oft recurring instructions in the DDC (from the 18th edition onwards): "Add to . . . the numbers following. . . ." In CC it is usually used whenever an isolate requires differentiation on a subject basis. Wherever (SD) is to be used, very clear instructions have been provided either in the schedules or sometimes in the corresponding rules. Even, if not instructed the situations where it can be employed are strikingly suggestive. It may be used to sharpen or to create anew the isolate number in any of the facets. A great deal of discretion should be used in applying the (SD). There is no difficulty in knowing where to apply (SD), but certainly in how to use it. If not instructed properly, one is always at a loss whether the (SD) being used should come as [P] or [E]—both of them seem equal contenders.

For example (SD) has been used as personality in 24 Special Libraries, D6, 8 Electrical Engineering, R4 Ethics, S4 Vocational Psychology, T : 3 Teaching Method, X8 Industry, V : 19 Foreign Policy, and Z Law.

24 (Z)	Law libraries
D6, 8(B)	Computers
S4 (L)	Psychology of Doctors
V44 : 19(X)	India's Foreign Economic Policy
X8 (J)	Agricultural Economics
Y73 (Q7)	Muslim Society
Z(Q6)	Christian Law
T : 3(B)	Teaching of Mathematics
2 : 51, 9 (X)	Library Classification of Economics

In G : 3, [2M] is to be got by (SD)

Effect of Tea on the Living Organism
G : 3 ; (J451)

When a subject is applied over another, then it comes as Energy Isolate.

Philosophy of Education
T : (R)
Educational Psychology
T : (S)

Mathematics, Philosophy, Law and sometimes Sociology, usually form Energy (SD), as these are taken as methodologies involving some action or problem :

Mathematical Economics
X : (B)
Philosophy of History
V : (R)
Labour Laws
X : 9 : (Z)
Biophysics
G : (C)
Biophysics of the Eyes
G, 185 : (C)
Mathematical Biophysics
G : (C) : (B)

As also said in the chapter on geographical isolates, the space isolate may also be sharpened by (SD)

1 (Q7)	Muslim countries
5 (Q7)	Muslim Europe
44 (P152)	Hindi Speaking States of India
4 (Y : 52)	Over populated countries of Asia

It may also be taken care that the isolate proposed to be got or sharpened by (SD) is not enumerated already. For example, at the outset one may be tempted to synthesise the class number U : (B) for Mathematical Geography. But having a glance on the schedule one finds it as U1, so the synthesised class number is wrong. Similarly one may make the class number for the Psychology of Engineer as S(D), which is wrong and S4 (D) is correct. Similarly for Religious Libraries, the number is 24(Q) and not 2(Q). This much care must be exercised, as the schedule is the final authority.

(3) Geographical Device

The Geographical Device (GD) is said to be applied when a Geographical Isolate wholly or partly officiates as a personality facet. It means (GD) may be used either to sharpen an existing Personality Isolate or create altogether a new isolate by geographical characteristics.

In V History, Z Law, in canonical classes NA to NR of N Fine Arts, and z Generalia, personality is to be got by (GD) :

V44	Indian History
Z44	Indian Law
z44	Indology

In all the above class numbers "44" has been borrowed from the Space Isolates and obviously they are posing as Personality Isolates. Again :

NR44	Indian Music
NQ56	English Paintings
NA5	European Architecture

Here all the personality isolates have been got by (GD). (GD) is also used to sharpen some of the Personality Isolates in Q Religion, R Philosophy and Y Sociology. For example:

Q8	Other Religions (Divided by (GD) and by (FD))
Q8441	Sikhism

44 stands for India and the last digit 1 has been got by Favoured Category Device.

In Philosophy, R8 Other Systems of Philosophy are to be got by (GD). For example :

Greek Philosophy
R851
Chinese Philosophy
R841

Here 51 and 41 respectively have been taken from the Geographical Isolates.

Y74-79 Territorial Divisions to be got by (GD).

Indian Society
Y744

Here Y7 has been amplified by (GD), i.e., 44 taken from the schedule of Geographical Isolates.

Similarly,

Sociology of Americans will be :
Y773

In P Linguistics, [P_2] is to be sharpened by (GD).

Chhatisgarhi Dialect of Hindi
P152, 9D447185
Pakistani Dialect of Punjabi
P153, 9D44Q7

Here [P_2] 9D has been sharpened by 4452 and 44Q7 respectively.

(GD) and (CD) may also be used in succession to form a Personality Isolate: For example :

UNO History
V1N4

Here 1 got by (GD) has further been sharpened by (CD).

Similarly

V1N48 History of British Commonwealth

In Common Isolates k cyclopaedia, m periodical, n serial, p conference proceedings, v history and w Biography [P_1] is to be got by (GD).

k56, L. Encyclopaedia Britannica.

Collected Biographies of Indian Scientists (youngest born in 1935)
Aw44, N3

(5th) International Study Conference on Classification (Canada, 1991)
2 : 51p1, N91

Here p has been sharpened by 1 taken from the schedule of Space Isolates.

Indian Journal of Sociology
Ym44, N

Here m has been sharpened first by (GD) viz. 44 standing for India and taken from the Geographical Isolates.

All such situations where (GD) is to be applied have been indicated in the schedules. There seems hardly any place where we have to apply (GD) of our own.

(4) Alphabetical Device

It consists in either sharpening or forming a new isolate number on the basis of its nomenclature. For sharpening an isolate number it is used to individualize trade names, of commercial products and cultivars in agriculture. For example :

D5125A	Atlas Bicycle
D5125AV	Avon Bicycle
D5125H	Hero Bicycle
D5135R	Rajdoot Motor Cycle
J381B	Basmati Rice
J381P	Parmal Rice

while using the (AD), only the minimum number of Roman Alphabets should be used to individualize the isolate number.

In case of Personality Posteriorising Common Isolates, [P_1] is to be got by (AD) in case of local institutions.

Guru Nanak Dev University
T4.4443, d, G

(Here G stands for Guru Nanak Dev University)

Holy Heart Elementary Kindergarten School Amritsar
TL8, 15.4443. A,d,H

[P_4] of O Literature can also be got by (AD). It is an option, but it is easy and therefore widely accepted :

Shakespeare's Hamlet
O111, 2J64, H

Shakespeare's As You Like It
O111, 2J64, A

G.B. Shaw's Arms and the Man
O111, 2M56, A

Also in N Fine Arts, the (AD) may be used to individualize the works of different artists belonging to the same school. Further the works of an artist may also be individualized by (AD).

Collected Paintings of Picaso
NQ52, NxP

P stands for Picaso, N is by (CD)
Again

Picaso's *Guernica*
NQ52, NxP, G

Alphabetical Device is applied as the last resort; as this sort of arrangement, as Ranganathan himself says, is least helpful though easy to handle and use.

(5) Mnemonic Device

It means that when the same concept recurs in different parts of the schedule, it should be denoted by the same digits. For example,

Animal Physiology
K : 3

Plant Physiology
I : 3

Human Physiology
L : 3

But in the CC the mnemonic device has attained intuitive depths, and entities which are seminally the same or analogous, should also be represented by the same digits :

Human Diseases
L : 4
Social ills
Y : 4

Indeed, it is very difficult to perceive the seminally equivalent entities, therefore, it is very difficult to apply the mnemonic device. It is mostly used by the classificationist, and very rarely by the classifier. Nevertheless, it imparts a uniformity, symmetry and a formulable structure to the scheme. The list of seminally equivalent entities has been given in Rule 05841 page 1.32 of the Rules.

(6) Classic Device

Classics, we know, are works embodying startling innovations and create new paradigms in Alfred Kuhn's words. A Classic stands the test of time and always provokes commentaries and further commentaries upon it. To keep a text and the critical books on it together, Ranganathan devised what he calls the Classic Device (ClD).

It consists in putting the digit x after the ultimate class to which a classic belongs. The digit x is further amplified by [P_1] and [P_2] which stand for the Author facet and the Work facet respectively. NO COMMA IS INSERTED BETWEEN x AND [P_1].

[P_1] is got by favoured category Device for the first 16 classical authors belonging to that ultimate class; and for the rest [P_1] may be got by (CD) as in O Literature. [P_2] is also got as the work facet as in [P_4] of O Literature. It may be got by Group Notation or by (AD). Commentary and further Commentaries are also treated as Personality facets. The formula takes the form :

[Class number] x [Author], [Work], [Commentary], [Sub-commentary]

Some examples borrowed from Part 3 of the CC, will illustrate the above formula.

Caraka Samhita
LBx1, 1

It means that it is the first work of the first author on Ayurveda.

Susruta Samhita
LB : 4 : 7x2, 1

It is a work on Ayurvedic Surgery (LB:4:7) by an author who is deemed to be the second classical author on the subject and it is his first work.

(7) Favoured Category Device (FD)

This device maintains that entities having the same function may be distinguished by their popularity, use, or the literary warrant—actually all three means the same thing. Of such entities a list is drawn in the order of their popularity and the entity at the top is given the number 1, the second 2 and so on, which is added to the penultimate isolate number.

This device has been employed in J Agriculture. For example, all the seed foods have the class numbers J 38. Further, kinds of foodgrains whether rice, wheat, etc., are distinguished on the basis of their popularity of use :

J381	Rice
J 382	Wheat
J 383	Oats
J 384	Rye

Apart from this, as also stated earlier, the favoured category device is used to get the isolate number for a classical author. It is also used in case of Personality Isolates in Q Religion got by (FD). Actually it is more a classificationist's rationale than a classifier's device.

(8) Superimposition Device

Especially in depth classification work, the focus of an isolate may be distributed over more than one isolate of the same facet. Therefore, in the CC, two different isolates from the same facet may join, yet not form a complex class. For example, in the main class Sociology, the isolate for "Urban Woman" has not been enumerated. But both "Urban" and "Woman" occur as different isolates in the Personality of Y Sociology. There is no relation between the two—except that in this particular title they complement one another. So the phase relation cannot be applied here. In such cases the isolate number is constructed by the mutual denudation of two or more isolates within the same facet by the Superimposition Device (SID).

Ranganathan defines (SID) as "connecting together two or more isolate ideas belonging to the same universe of isolate ideas".[3] It consists in putting a hyphen "-" between the two or more isolates involved. For example, the "Urban Woman" will thus get the class numbers:

Y 15-33

It is a question that which of the two isolates should come first. The simple rule is that, the isolate which occurs first should come first. But if such a sequence is unintelligible then the sequence may be reversed. For example :

Female University Students
T 4-55

Though in the CC there are no examples showing more than two isolates connected together by (SID), but in the rules or otherwise there is nothing to prevent us to construct isolate number by (SID) involving three or more isolates :

Genius Female University Student
T 4-55-61

Urban working class youth
Y 12-33-49

National Library of Medicine (USA)
213-4 (L).73

National Science Library of India
213-4 (A).44

Another significant use of (SID) occurs in constructing isolate number for Space Isolates numbers for colonial empires :

British Empire
1-56

French Colonies in the World
1-53

Similarly

Italian Possessions in Africa
6-52

British India
44-56

(Please note that here 56-44 will be an absurd isolate number)

Though (SID) is a great hospitality device, yet its too much use shows some snags in the enumeration pattern. If in a main class too many isolates are got by (SID), it shows lack of foresight on the part of the classificationist. Ranganathan informs that this device will be used too frequently in the seventh edition of the scheme, as that will be a really depth classification schedule.

Important

In the *Prolegomena* (Sec. RP_1) Ranganathan states that "Superimposition of isolate ideas is most commonly experienced in a Personality Facet". Therefore, its use in other rounds and levels of Personality should be avoided. Moreover, in other categories such as Matter, Energy, and Time, the (SID) should not be used. Anyhow, the following class number is admissible.

Eye Tissues of Children
L 9 C, 12-185

But the following class number is NOT ADMISSIBLE

Poetic Drama of T.S. Eliot
O111, 1-2 M 88

And Say "Distribution Management in Coal Industry"
X 8 (F 551) : 3-8

is also wrong, as (SID) is not possible in the Energy category.

REFERENCES

1. CC (6th ed) Rule 05813, page 1.29.
2. CC (6th ed) Rule 05814, page 1.29.
3. *Prolegomena* Sec. PF 2.

5

MAIN CLASS, CANONICAL CLASS AND AMPLIFIED MAIN CLASS

Basic class is a subject without any isolate idea. Broadly speaking these are of four kinds : Main classes, Canonical classes, Systems and Specials. Concept of a main class is traditional ; and canonical classes are traditional divisions of a main class. No subject or document is without a basic class, it means that a main class or a canonical class is always present in a subject. But a subject may be treated wholly from a particular viewpoint or a school of thought. For example, Relativity Theory or Newtonian Principles in Physics. These are known as Systems and considered as the first kind of a amplified main class. A subject may also be studied in a very narrow field of specialization. Here the field of study is very intensive instead of being extensive. For example, Low temperature Physics or Plasma Physics in the main class physics or Child medicine in main class Medical Science. These are known as Specials and treated as second kind of a Amplified main class.

Systems and Specials

Systems : Different approaches to a common end are termed as systems. Various schools of thoughts emerge due to lack of communication between different working groups. They are also the result of different opinions adhered to. To represent all these viewpoints or systems Ranganathan has devised a very neat and mechanical method. It is simply done by amplification of the ultimate class number by the (CD)—the epoch of origin of that system. *But the most favoured system is not represented by (CD)—by the application of the Favoured Category Device.* The (CD) is applied subject to the rules for (CD) regarding the epoch to be used in constructing the time focus. These rules have been given in Secs. 05811 to 05817 pages 1.29 to 1.30 of the Rules portion.

These rules in a nutshell mean that only minimum number of digits should be used to individualize.

Usually the Systems occur at the level of a main class and in such cases, the Systems may also occur at the Canonical class level or even at the level of isolates.

For example : In Psychology

SM	Experimental Psychology
SN	Gestalt Psychology
SN8	Field Psychology

In Education

TL	Rousseau's School
TL7	Herbert's School
TL8	Kindergarten School

In Economics

XB	War Economics
XM2	Socialism
XN	Communism

Examples of systems occurring at the canonical class levels :

B6M	Non-Euclidean Geometry
B6M3	Elliptic Geometry
B6N	Line-Complex Geometry

Examples of Systems at the Isolate Level :

Corpuscular Theory of Light
C5:8K

Wave Theory of Light
C5:8K9

Quantum Theory of Light
C5:8N

Similarly in Library Science various cataloguing codes and classification schemes are to be considered as Systems:

Classification
2 : 51

Dewey Decimal Classification
2 : 51M

Universal Decimal Classification
2 : 51M96

Colon Classification
2 : 51N3

It may be interesting to note that *neither* all the systems are got by (CD) *nor* all the class numbers got by (CD) correspond to Systems. For examples, in R philosophy the Systems are got by (GD). And the following class numbers are not Systems, but pseudo-subject device class numbers.

MB1	Calculating Machines
MY2	Athletics
G : 33C6	Electrical Effect in Metabolism

Systems occur in B Mathematics, C Physics, J Agriculture, L Medicine, S Psychology, T Education V : 91 Election Systems, and X Economics. Places where they occur have been indicated in the schedules, others can be got by (CD):

Osteopathy System of Medicine
LM 7

Specials: The term "Special" in the CC stands for field of specialization by restricting the area of study. Restriction in area is counter-balanced by the depth studies. For Example, in medicine :

Paediatrics
Industrial Medicine
Sports Medicine
Tropical Medicine

In Agriculture :

Dry Farming
Soil Farming

In Economics :

Small Scale Industry
Private Enterprise
Public Utility

These are denoted by amplifying the main class digit by 9 followed by another Roman Capital letter

Specials in Economics	X9A
Small Scale Economy	X9B
Public Enterprise	X9W
Specials in Medicine	L9A

Embryo	L9B
Child	L9C
Tropical Medicine	L9H

The alphabetical digit after "9" is either got by (AD) or by pseudo subject device or is purely arbitrary.

Rules : When a personality facet follows a System or Special facet or both, then a comma must precede it. And if both the System and Special facets are present then the System facet should form the earlier facet followed respectively by the Special facet and the Personality facet. A comma should be put between the System facet and the Personality facet; and between the Special facet and the Personality facet, to remind again. Thus the formula, in general is :

(Sm F), (Sp F), [P]

Homeopathic treatment of eye diseases

LL, 185 : 4 : 6

(Here only System facet is present)

Homeopathic treatment of the eye diseases of children

LL, 9 C, 185 : 4 : 6

When both the System and Special facets occur simultaneously, the digit for the main class is not to be repeated with Special facet, as it has already been represented in the System facet.

Some more examples will clarify the use of Systems and Specials :

Treatment of children diseases

L9C : 4 : 6

Treatment of the eye disease of children

L9C, 185 : 4 : 6

Small Scale Production

X9B : 2

Small Scale Textile Production

X 9 B, 8 (M 7) : 2

Small Scale Cooperative Production of Textiles

XM, 9B, 8(M 7) : 2

Psycho-analytic study of Boys' Intelligence

SM9,21 : 72

A book dealing with two or more systems or specials, should be amplified by A only.

Specializations in Medicine

L 9 A

Various Systems of Medicine

L A

Treatment of eye diseases of children and females
L9A, 185 : 4 : 6

Treatment of eye diseases of children and females according to different systems of medicine
LA, 9A, 185 : 4 : 6

Specials occur in the main classes E, G, J, L and X.

6

COMPLEX CLASSES

I

At the outset, one may be reminded that the terms "Basic class", "Complex Class" and "Compound Class" are distinct terms having precisely defined meanings in the CC. Therefore, these should be used with discrimination. A compound class is any Basic class attached with one or more isolates. For example :

L185	Eye Medicine
L : 4	Human Diseases
L185 : 4	Eye Diseases
L185 : 4 : 6	Treatment of eye diseases.

All these are compound classes. They are infinite in number.

A complex class is defined as a class comprising of two (or more) phases taken either from the same main class or different main classes. These phases are locked in some inter-relation which are five in number. The device to construct a complex class is known as Phase Relation Device. It brings hospitality in array. It is a very efficient Device to cope with the turbulent outturn of inter-disciplinary subjects. Though Ranganathan is not the first to provide a class number for the inter-relation of two different subjects, (UDC did earlier to him) but certainly CC is the only scheme which handles such subjects with a mathematical precision.

At the first instance, in the 6th edition (1963) of the CC, Ranganathan recognizes five kinds of relations or interactions between the involved phases. Namely these are :

(1) General Relation

It is a relation comprehending all other relations not included in any of the following four relations. This sort of relation is vague and undefined. For example, Relations of Political Science with History.

(2) Bias Relation

When the exposition of a phase is favourable to or inclined towards another phase, it is deemed to be a Bias Relation. For example, Mathematics for Biologists, Psychology for Doctors, or Physics for Civil Engineers, are all examples of Bias Phase Relations.

(3) Comparison Relation

When the involved phases are compared with one another, then it is called a Comparison Relation, e.g., Physics compared with Chemistry.

(4) Difference Relations

As the name implies, this type of relation involves the exposition of the difference between the involved phases. For example, Difference between the Indian Constitution and the British Constitution; Difference between Mysticism and Metaphysics.

(5) Influencing Relation

When the phases are so involved that one is influencing the exposition of the other, it is termed as the Influencing Relation. For example, the Influence of British Constitution on the Indian Constitution : Influence of Mathematics on Physics.

Levels of Relations

This is not all to be more precise. To make class numbers brief, Ranganathan has differentiated each of the five relations into **three levels**, viz., whether they occur at the level of the main class, facets or isolates.

Inter Subject Phase Relation

When phases involved in the phase relation belong to two different main classes, it is termed as Phase Relation. For example :

Difference between Mysticism and Religion.
(It is a case of intra-phase difference relation)
Law for Sociologists
(It is a case of intra-phase Bias Relation)

Relation between History and Literature
(It is a case of intra-phase General Relation)
Influence of Chemistry on Technology
(Intra-phase Influencing Relation).

Intra-Facet Relation

When the two phases belong to one and the same main class, same category, but to different arrays within the same facet of the same category, it is termed as Intra-Facet Relation. For example, difference between Hindu and Muslim religions :

Here both Hindu and Muslim religions belong to the personality facet of the main class Q Religion, but their arrays are different.

Similarly, let us take the example of the title "Influence of Transport on Trade". Both Transport and Trade belong to the Energy facet of X Economics, but belong to the different arrays.

They are again of five kinds ranging from general to influencing relations.

Some more examples are :

A Comparative study of Indian and British Laws.
(It is a case of Intra-Facet Comparison Relation)
Anatomy for Physiologists.
(Intra-Facet Bias Relation)

Intra-Array Relations

Ranganathan has carried the division one step further by inventing what he calls Intra-Array Relations. In this case the two phases not only belong to the same facet of a main class, but also to the same array of that particular facet. In other words it is the relation between two equally ranked isolates whose immediate parents are the same.

For example : "Relation between the First and the Second House of the Indian Parliament". Here both the First and Second House belong to the same facet Personality and the same array 3 of [P_2] in V History. Thus it is a case of Intra-Array Relation. Further, it is a case of Intra-Array General Relation.

"Difference between the Education of Male and Female Students".

Since both the "Male" and "Female" belong to the 5th array in [P] of T Education, so it is a case of Intra-Array Difference Relation.

Comparison of English and French Pronunciations.

Here English and French belong to the same array in the Personality facet of P Linguistics. It is obviously a case of Intra-Array Comparison Relation.

They (Intra-Array Relations) are again of five kinds, like other levels of relations ranging from General to Influencing Relations.

Thus in all there are (5 × 3) 15 kinds of relations.

II

CONSTRUCTION OF A COMPLEX CLASS NUMBER

Having analysed the kind and level of the relation of two phases, it is not difficult to construct the class number for the complex subject. But prior to this, precedence of one phase over the other must be determined. Since the CC is a very standardized scheme, so the determination of the First and the Second Phase (Called Primary and Secondary Phase respectively) is vital. Ranganathan has formulated rigid but easy and unambiguous rules for this purpose.

(1) In case of General, Comparison and Difference Relations at any level, the Primary Phase is one with lesser ordinal value, i.e., which occurs first in the schedules. Accordingly, the Phase with higher ordinal value becomes the Secondary Phase. For example, in "Relation between Chemistry and Physics" C Physics forms the Primary Phase, while E Chemistry forms the Secondary Phase. Let us take another example. "Difference between Drama and Fiction". Here Drama is the Primary Phase and Fiction forms the Secondary Phase.

But in case of Bias and Influencing Phases determination of the First Phase is bit different and not as mechanical :

(1) In case of Bias Phase Relation the Biasing Phase, discriminating or Favouring Phase, forms the Primary Phase. To put it in other words, we can call it the donor or the active Phase. Accordingly the Favoured or discriminated phase becomes the Secondary Phase.

For example, "Mathematics for Engineers". Here Mathematics is the Biasing Phase, which is favouring or is the donor, so it is the Primary Phase; and therefore Engineering is the Secondary Phase. Similarly in "Law for Sociologists", Law is the Primary Phase. In "Sociology for Town Planners" and "Epistemology for Librarians". Sociology and Epistemology form the Primary Phases respectively.

Logic for such a rule is very simple. Mathematics whether it is for Engineers, Biologists or Psychologists, remains Mathematics *per se*, so it must go to the Mathematics Section, hence the Primary Phase.[1]

While in case of Influencing Relation, the above rule seems reversed. Here the Influenced Phase forms the Primary Phase and the influencing phase forms the Secondary Phase. Here the receiver is the First Phase.

For example, take the subject "Influence of *Bhagvadgita* on Hindi Literature". Here Hindi Literature is the influenced phase, so it will form the First Phase, and the *Bhagvadgita* is the Second Phase, as it is the influencing Phase. Again in the subject "Influence of Calculus on Physics", Physics is the First Phase and Calculus the Second Phase.[2]

Having determined the First and the Second Phases, connect the two phases by a zero and the specified relation indicator digit, which is always a roman small. Put the first phase, then a zero as a connecting symbol, and a roman small digit taken from chapter 6 of the schedule (page 2.28) followed by the notation for the Second Phase:

Phase I+0+a/y+Phase II

If there are common digits between Phase I and Phase II, these should be removed in Phase II.

Let us take examples one by one of every kind of Phase Relation:

Inter-Phase General Relation

Relation between Language and Literature
OoaP

Relation between 'Meteorology' and Ecological Environment
G : 550aU 28

Inter-Phase Bias Relation

Calculus for Physical Chemistry
B32 0b E : 2

Mathematics for Engineers
B 0b D

Inter-Phase Comparison Relation

Geography compared with Geology
H0cU

Inter-Phase Difference Relation

Difference between History and Political Science
V0dW

Difference between Biology and Biochemistry
E9G0dG

Inter-Phase Influencing Relation

Influence of Mathematics on Physics
C0gB

Impact of Computers on Research Libraries
236 0g D65,8(B)

Intra-Facet General Relation

Relation between Hinduism and Jainism
Q20j3

Intra-Facet Bias Relation

Epistemology for Logic
R2 0k 1

Intra-Facet Comparison Relation

Comparison of Racial Psychology and Social Psychology
S7 0m8

A Comparative Study of Shakespeare and George Bernard Shaw
O111, 2J64 0m M56

Intra-Facet Difference Relation

Difference between Gold and Paper currencies
X61;10n4

Intra-Facet Influencing Relation

Influence of Consumption on Production
X : 2or1

Intra-Array Relation

Intra-Array General Relation

Relation between University and Research Libraries
234 Ot6

Chemical Relation between Silver and Gold
E115 Ot8

Intra-Array Bias Relation

It seems that no viable or real example of such a relation is possible. However, following is a hypothetical case :

Functional Analysis for Nomography
B43 0u4

Intra-Array Comparison Relation

Comparison of Male and Female Curriculums in Education
T510v5 : 2

Comparison of Atomic Weights of Gold and Silver
E1150v8 : 14

Intra-Array Difference Relation

Difference between Refraction and Reflection of Light
C5 : 220w3

Difference between Circulation systems of University and College Libraries
2330w4 : 6

Intra-Array Influencing Relation

Influence of Temperature on Atmospheric Pressure
U2820y4

Influence of the opposition party on the party in office with regards to India's Home Policy
V44, 410y5 : 11

Some more examples :

Influence of Society on Scientific Research
A : f0gY

Science for Social Development
A 0bY : 7 : 7

International Seminar (2001) on Science for Social Development
A0bY : 7 : 7 p1, P01

Difference between the preparation of Basic Oxides and Acidic Oxides
E20n3 : 11

Difference between cataloguing of manuscripts in Academic and Business Libraries
230n4 ; 12 : 55

Relation between Telegraphy and Telephony
D65, 470t8

Comparison of English and French pronunciation
P1110v5 : 1

A social study of Difference between Urban and Rural Ornaments
Y310w3 : 86

In Analytical Chemistry a special form of Intra-Facet Bias Relation exists. The Rule E18 (page 1.76) reads, "In the case of analytical

Chemistry, an Intra-Facet Bias Isolate may be added in [P] using as its focus the number of the substance, whose presence in the original substance is being investigated by analysis". In other words, the substance to be estimated becomes the Secondary Phase, while the original compounds is the Primary Phase :

Quantitative analysis of Hydrogen in Water
E210 0k 110 : 34

Estimating by Physical methods the quantity of Zinc in an Alloy
E1930k23 : 34, B

(Though it seems as a Intra-Array Bias Phase Relation)

Detecting the presence of Hydrogen in Acids by X-ray Method
E30k110 : 33, E53

III

In all the above examples the number of phases have been limited to two only. There is no example in the CC where more than two phases exist. But in the rules for Phase Relation there is nothing which may prevent us to apply the rules to three or more Phases. For detailed discussion, see author's article in the *Herald of Library Science* V18 N4 (Oct. 1979) pp. 344-348.

REFERENCES

1. One may object to keeping a book "Mathematics for Engineers" among the mathematics books when it is specially written for Engineers. It seems, such a book will be more useful when placed with Engineering books. Since the CC is not a reader-oriented scheme but strictly a subject classification scheme, so a subject must file with its own class irrespective of its prospective readership considerations.
2. Rationale behind such a decision is simple. In the above examples Hindi Literature and Physics are respectively the subject proper and the Bhagvadgita and Calculus are simply effecting their exposition. Hence the rule.

7

PARALLEL SCHEDULES

Though it appears contrary to the definition, the "special isolates" strictly speaking, are not exclusively restricted to a single main class. Some of the isolates of a particular facet in a main class may also be borrowed wholly or partially by another main class. It is because every subject has many aspects, and in a particular main class its only single aspect is considered. The CC like other modern classifications is a discipline oriented system. So a subject gets scattered in different main classes. For example, take the term "Child". It may occur in the main classes psychology, education, sociology and even in medicine and Law. Take another example of the term "copper"; it occurs in chemistry, technology, geology, fine arts and economics. For brevity and simplicity of the schedules the classificationist enumerates such isolates only once. The classifier is directed to take the isolate from that main class (without the main class digit) whenever they are required in some other main class. Thus the classifier takes them as if they belong to the same main class. This device of parallel schedules secures automatic conformity to the canons of scheduled mnemonics and consistent sequence. It also endows the scheme with symmetry and a regulated structure.

A good example occurs in the (MC) 2 Library Science. Here the isolates in the matter facet have not been enumerated; instead we are instructed that these are the same as that of the [P] of a Generalia Bibliography. It means that notationally:

[M] of 2 Library Science=[P] of a Generalia Bibliography

Let us take the example "Cataloguing of Microfilms in a University Library". Its class number is 234; 1512: 55. Here isolate number 1512 in [M] has been borrowed from the [P] of a Generalia Bibliography, where al512 denotes Bibliography of Microfilms.

Ranganathan in his *Prolegomena* (Ed. 3, Sec. KC2 p. 298) mentions that there are seventy six such cases of parallel schedules. These may be divided into the following categories:

(1) *Scheduled Mnemonics* : Some terms or concepts if occurring under different main classes are denoted by the same digits. For example the [E] cum [2P] isolates of the main classes G Biology, I Botany and K Zoology are almost the same, so have been enumerated only once under the first occurring main class G. For the [E] cum [2P] isolates of I Botany and K Zoology, the classifier has to refer back to the main class G Biology.

Physiology G : 3
Plant Physiology I : 3
Animal Physiology K : 3

Another example of this kind occurs in NQ Paintings, [P_3] of NQ is the same as that of [P_3] of ND Sculpture:

Human Paintings
NQ, 1

Here [P_3] 1 has been got from the [P_3] of ND Sculpture. Another striking example occurs in W Political Science. Here the isolates in [P_2] and [E] are exactly the same as the [P_2] and [E] respectively of V History.

Political Parties—a historical study
V, 4

Political Parties—an academic study
W, 4

Functions of the Head of a State—a political study
W, 1 : 3

Here [E] 3 has been borrowed from the [E] of V History.

(2) *Cases where the isolates are partially same:* H1 Mineralogy has some [P] isolates exclusively of its own, while the rest are to be borrowed from the [P] of E Chemistry. For example :

Mineralogy of Gold
H1118

H1 is the canonical class Mineralogy, while [P] 118 has been got from the [P] of E Chemistry.

Similarly [P] of F Technology is also the same as in E Chemistry, though F Technology has also some [P] isolates especially of its own:

Acid Technology
F3

(3) *Mutation of Facets:* This type of parallel schedules pertain to the cases where one facet when borrowed by another main class mutates into a different facet. Obvious example is that the [P_2] of K Zoology and KZ Animal Husbandry are the same as [P] of L Medicine.

Eye diseases of dogs
KZ 541, 185 : 4

Here [P_2] 185 has been taken from [P] of L Medicine.
Similarly,

Insect legs
K86, 134

Here [P_2] 134 has been borrowed from the [P] of L Medicine. Another such example, as already said, pertains to the [M] of 2 Library Science which is to be taken from [P] of a Generalia Bibliography. Another striking example is [2M] in G : 3 Physiology and its sub-divisions. Here [2M] is to be taken from the [P] of E Chemistry.

Sulphur metabolism in plants
I : 33 ; 161
Oxygen physiology in animals
K : 3 ; 160

Here [2M] 161 and 160 respectively have been borrowed from the [P] of E Chemistry.

(4) Cases where one isolate is sharpened like another isolate in the same or some other main class.

(4A) *Different Main Classes:* In the (MC) Y Sociology Y6 Sociology of Abnormal and defective people is to be divided as S6 Abnormal Psychology.

A social study of blind people
Y68
A social study of insanes
Y63

In this category there are also cases where an isolate is divided like the division of a whole category in another main class. For example in a Generalia Bibliography a8 is to be further subdivided as the [P] of Y Sociology.

Bibliography of children books
a811

Here the digit pair 11 has been borrowed from the [P] of Y Sociology where Y11 is children sociology. Similarly,

Bibliography of books for rural people
a831

State control of edible oils
L : 523943

Here the last three digits 943 have been taken from the [P] of F Technology, as per instructions. It is also a case of mutation of facets as the [E] in L Medicine has been divided like the [P] of F Technology.

Bibliography of books in Devnagri script
a2152

Here a2 has been subdivided by the language taken from the language schedule.

Another example is in D8 Sanitary Engineering. Here D8533 Chemical Treatment is to be divided by the substance taken from the [P] of E Chemistry.

Chlorınation of water (for purification)
D8553 171

In this case the last three digits 171 come from the [P] of E Chemistry where E171 is chlorine. *Majority of the parallel schedules belong to this kind.*

(4B) Division (Sharpening) like another isolate in the same main class:

This kind of borrowing is not only restricted to amongst the different main classes : an isolate may be further subdivided like another isolate in the same main class. For example—

G : 341	Inanition
G : 345	Water Fasting
G : 346	Fasting

Here each of the three class numbers can be further subdivided as G : 33 Metabolism. For example,

Fasting anabolism
G : 3461

Physical effect of fasting
G : 346C

Chemical effect of inanition
G : 341E

Another such example occurs in P Linguistics: Here [P_3] 16 voiced consonant is to be divided like [P_3] 15 consonant :

Circular voiced consonants in English language
P111, 162

Bilabial voiced consonants
P, 168

In R Philosophy, the other aspects of Indian Philosophy R6, 9 are to be got like the divisions of R from R1 to R5. For example,

Indian epistemology (Theory of)
R6, 92

Where R2 is Epistemology

Family ethics in Indian Philosophy
R6, 942

Where R42 is Family ethics

Similarly,

Indian theory of aesthetics
R6, 95

as R5 is Aesthetics

(5) *Modified Parallel Schedule:* These are of two kinds.

(5A) *Modified Parallel Isolates:* In this case the isolate borrowed from another main class is not used as such but modified a little. For example, energy isolates of F Technology are the same as the subdivisions of E : 8 Chemical manipulation. It means that in case of [E] of F Technology, the digit 8 is to be omitted from the subdivisions of E : 8, so that the isolate number begins with the second digit onwards. For example,

Industrial distillation
F : 35

Industrial filtration
F : 92

Another example of the kind occurs in H6 Paleontology, where the Time isolates are not taken from the common schedule of time isolates. Instead it is to be taken from H5 Stratigraphy by replacing H5 by A.

Silurian aves
H696‘A23

Here time facet has been got by substituting A for H5, as the Silurian stratigraphy is H523. Similarly,

Cainozoic vermes
H66‘A4

(5B) *Modified Parallel Schedules where the terms are modified:* Instead of adapting the notation, here the terms are modified to connote meaning as per the local immediate context. For example, in Y Sociology,

[2E] for 5 of [E] are the same as [2E] of 4 [E] of Y sociology, but with suitable terminology:

Prevention of social evils
Y : 44 : 5

where [2E] 5 means prevention. But when as per instruction the [2E] 5 is borrowed for Y : 5 and its subdivisions, the term will change its terminology, though essentially its meaning will remain seminally the same. For example:

Y : 52 : 5 Control of overpopulation

Here [2E] 5 has changed its meaning to "control" in this context.

Even if not instructed, sometimes the terms may be modified to suit the occasion.

Principal of a secondary school
T2 : 87

In T : 8 Educational Management 8 is to be subdivided as X : 8 Business Management. But in X : 8 there is no term as "Principal". Therefore in the educational management context, the term X : 87 Executive has been adapted to mean a Principal. In case of a school it would mean Headmaster and in the context of a University it may mean Vice-Chancellor.

Similarly [P_2] isolates of K Zoology and KZ Animal Husbandry have to be taken from the [P] of L Medicine. But in some cases, we may have to change the terminology, as there is no complete identity between human organs and animal organs. For example:

Aves wings
K96, 163

Since human beings have no wings and the analogous organ is the arm, so [P_2] has been borrowed from L163.

It may also be taken as a case of modified parallel schedule where terminology is modified so that [P_2] and [E] of a Personality [PCI] digit are the same as that of V History.

Functions of the President of Indian Library Association
2.44, g, 9N3, 1 : 3

Here [E] 3 and the preceding digit 1 which is [P_2] of the (ACI) g have been borrowed from [E] and [P_2] of V History respectively.

Here are some more examples of the cases of parallel schedules. Examples have been taken at random without any thought of the kinds described above.

Classification of precious stones
H19 : 11

Cold storage of eggs
KZ351 : 75 : 84

Electric railway carriage
D66, 4153

(Here 153 has been borrowed from D5 153 as per instructions)

Chemical effect of water fasting in plants
I : 345 E

Physical effect of inanition
G : 341 C

Fasting katabolism in animals
K : 3462

Let us now take a very interesting example of **double parallelism.** Δ, 2 "Spiritual experience about Nature" is to be further subdivided as in [P_3] of ND Sculpture. Therefore:

Spiritual experience about sky
Δ, 28

which can further be subdivided as B9 Astronomy.

Spiritual experience about Moon
Δ, 282

Here the last digit 2 has been borrowed from B9 where B92 is Moon.

We can, similarly multiply such examples to a large extent. Wherever an isolate is divided further like another isolate, adequate instructions exist for the purpose. In no case it is to be applied at classifier's initiative. In that case, either of the Subject Device, Superimposition Device or the Phase Relation Device may help to get a co-extensive class number. Therefore, the device of parallel schedules must be distinguished from all these devices to combine two or more isolates. It is rather more subtle than the (SD) and obviously secures brevity in notation. It is exactly analogous to "As" instructions in the UDC.

8

DIFFERENTIAL FACETS

As per definition and necessity of a faceted scheme, it is expected that the different facets are combinable with one another in the prescribed sequence. An isolate from one facet can be combined meaningfully with any other isolate from a different facet. This is what happens mostly in Ranganathan's Colon Classification. This characteristic alone increases manifold the capacity and hospitality of the scheme.

This characteristic of combination is true as long as all the isolates in the primary facet have the same secondary and tertiary facets. It only means that all the isolates in the personality facet should have the same parts (denoted by levels of [P] and problems (denoted by [E]). But in this age of specialisation many isolates may develop their own peculiarities—both in parts and action. Therefore, the isolates denoting specialised entities may combine meaning fully only with a particular isolate from another facet. This secondary facet having a limited combining capacity is called a **differential facet**—they differ from isolate to isolate. For example.

D2 Irrigation and drainage work has its own special [P_2] isolates as follows:

1. Source
2. Headwork
3. Surplus work

   . . . .

8. Flood protecting and river training work.

Above [P_2] isolates are only applicable to D2, not to D3 or D4 and so on. Therefore, this above isolate group is called a differential facet of D2. We can also call them doubly special isolates as their specialisation has increased one step further.

Though this tendency seems detrimental or contrary to the spirit of a faceted scheme, but in an age of increasing specialisation it is quite inevitable.

The doubly special isolates or the differential facets occur in many main classes of the CC schedules. Wherever differential facets exist, an accompanying note indicates the restricted area of their application. For example, another tangible example occurs in E Chemistry. [P_2] isolates also occur here but are not applicable to every [P_1] isolates in E Chemistry. [P_2] of E Chemistry is only meaningful for E5, E6, E7 and E8. Therefore, if these [P_2] isolates are combined with any isolate from E1 to E4, and E9 it will not be meaningful. For example:

Organic acids
E5, 3

But the following number is *not admissible*

Nitrogen compounds of hydrogen
E 110, 5

Because [P_2] isolates of E Chemistry have no jurisdiction over E1 isolates.

In case of KZ Animal Husbandry, every [E] has its different [2P] isolates.

Feeding grass to horses
KZ 442 : 1 (J 251)

Here [2P] has been got by (SD) as per instructions.

But in case of

KZ : 4 Animal diseases

[2P] is the same as for L : 4.

For example,

Infectious diseases of animals
KZ : 42

Here 2 of 42 is [2P].

[2P] isolates for KZ : 7 are different from other [2P] isolates. Not only this, they also vary according to [P] of KZ—a case which may be termed as a doubly differential facet:

Cow butter milk
KZ 311 : 75
Hen eggs
KZ 35 : 75

Here 2P [5] has changed meanings depending on [P].

"P, 15 consonants" and their isolates have a special schedule of Common Isolates. These "Common Isolates" are not applicable anywhere except to these:

Plosive circular consonants
P, 15201

But to make the following *class number is wrong*

P, 1103 Rolled vowels

as 03 common isolate cannot be applied to P, 11.

In case of R Indian Philosophy [P_2] isolates are only applicable from R65 to R6893. The [P_2] isolates are not applicable to R61 to R645.

In case of S Psychology [2E] cum [3P] isolates are only applicable to S : 2 and S : 3.

In case of T Education [2P2] facet, which usually represent the technique, vary from energy to energy isolate. For example, T : 3 has its own set of [2P2] isolates while T : 4 has its own different set of [$2P_2$] isolates, and so on. For example,

Teaching Physics by audio-visual methods
T : 3 (C), 1
Home work in Physics
T : 4 (C), 1

Here [$2P_2$] 1 has different meanings depending upon the energy isolate—hence a differential facet.

In case of X Economics matter facet is only applicable for X61, and not to any other personality isolates. Similarly X62 and X72 have their own different energy isolates enumerated at the end of all the general energy isolates of X Economics.

X8 (F182) : 2	Iron production
X627 : 2	Saving Bank's reserves
X722 : 2	Exemption from property tax
X625 : 11	Rate of interest in commercial banks
X722 : 11	Equal taxation in property tax

Here [E] has different meanings depending on the personality isolate.

In Z Law, [P_3] isolates vary from isolate to isolate in [P_2] facet.

Z44, 2, 2	Law of possession of property in India
Z44, 3, 2	Form of contact in Indian Law

Here [P_3] 2 varies in meaning depending upon [P_2]. Similarly [P_4] in Z Law is only applicable to [P_3] 7 : and [E] cum [2P] isolates are only applicable to [P_2] 98 and not to any other facet.

Canonical classes can also be viewed as varied form of differential facets. Every canonical class falling within a main class has its own set of personality, matter and energy isolates:

C3 : 3	Sound frequency
C4 : 3	Thermometry
C6 : 3	Electric potential

Here meaning of 3 in [E] varies from canonical class to canonical class.

This catalogue of Differential facets as existing in the CC is not exhaustive. Examples of various shades of differential facets can be considerably multiplied.

Uses

Use of differential facets narrows down the area of the applicability, so it takes less time in locating the required isolate from the schedules. Therefore, it also avoids unnecessary complications. In other words it adds to the simplicity of the scheme.

A big advantage of such a method is that it secures **brevity in notation**. Because for a differential facet whole range of digits from 0 to 9 are available, so here the base of notation is quite wider. Hence a shorter notation for the differential facet isolates. Thus the method of differential facets has a solution to the burning problem of our day—the increasing length of class number. This also increases the hospitality of the scheme. These areas need to be exploited for such gains.

But there may be some confusion while retranslating the class number in natural language, say for chain indexing. One may inadvertently look for general isolates instead of the specially special ones. From a class number it is never clear whether a particular isolate is a case of a differential facet or is from a general one.

FURTHER READING

Maltby, Arthur, *Sayers' Manual of Classification for Librarians*, 5th ed., London, Andre Deutsch, 1975, p. 92.

9

FILING SEQUENCE

Since the CC uses a mixed notation, therefore, the filing order of the class number poses some problems. It is considered as a complicated process to the extent that this factor alone has deterred many potential users from using it in their libraries. The ordinal value of each species is not written on its face, as it happens in the case of a pure notation. Indicator digits have further complicated the problem. Ranganathan has fixed the ordinal (sequential) value of each digit according to use. Generally speaking the indicator digits have the least ordinal value and the Roman Capitals have the highest value. Lower case alphabets have the ordinal value more than any of the indicator digits, but among the substantive digits they have the least value. Ordinal value of the Indo-Arabic numbers lies between the Roman Small and the Roman Capital alphabets. Since the CC follows the **Principle of Inversion**, so the ordinal value of the indicator digits increases in reverse order of the PMEST order. It means that of the principal five indicator digits the inverted comma " ' " has the lowest ordinal value, while the comma "," has the highest ordinal value. However, the ordinal value of each digit is given below in the strict order of their increasing ordinal value (Rule 025, p. 1.6):

) ← → 0 ' . : ; , - a/z 0/9 A/M Δ N/Z (

Ranganathan has fixed different values of two different parts of a parenthesis. Arrestor has the least value, whereas the starter has the highest value of all the digits, i.e., more than Z. Arrestor is followed by the backward arrow and a forward arrow. It may be noted that the zero has two ordinal values depending upon its role. As a phase relation indicator digit it lies between the forward arrow and the inverted comma— the indicator digit for time. As a Indo-Arabic numeral it has ordinal value more than z but less than 1. Hyphen, the symbol for (SID) has the highest value of all the indicator digits except the starter. The value of

Δ (Greek Delta) has been fixed to lie between M and N. It may be noted all the numerals 0/9 are decimal fractions.

A queer rule regarding ordinal values is that any class number or digit followed by an (ACI) digit or an arrow will have precedence over itself. In other words when any digit is followed by a Roman small, or an arrow then its ordinal value is decreased, so it will have precedence over itself (Rule 0251, page 1.6). For example:

2 : 51	Classification
2 : 51k	Dictionary of classification

of these two class numbers, the class number 2 : 51k will come earlier to 2 : 51. Similarly Bm will come earlier to B on the shelves or in classified catalogue.

Similarly attaching of any of the two arrows decreases the ordinal value of the class number. Therefore, B'N → has lesser ordinal value than B'N.

To repeat, the ordinal value of the indicator digits has been so fixed that it helps to arrange class numbers in the order of their increasing concreteness. But the sequence of facets within a facet formula is in the reverse order, i.e., in the order of decreasing concreteness. It is known as the **Principle of Inversion**. This inversion principle is also followed by the UDC. This inversion principle is used to secure an overall order of increasing concreteness.

It may further be noted that it is all due to the different ordinal value of the indicator digits that the documents are arranged in an Apupa pattern. As the left handed penumbral subjects are due to the (ACI)s and right handed penumbral subjects are due to the (PCI)s—which have different ordinal values. A sequence of class numbers is given by way of illustrations:

2k	Encyclopaedia of Library Science
2	Library Science
20bT	Libraries for Education
2'N →	Future of Libraries
2'N	Contemporary Libraries
2 : 51	Classification
2 : 51'N	Classification in the 20th century
2 ; 17	Maps in Libraries
2 ; 17 : 51	Classification of Maps
2 ; 17 : 51.44	Classification of Maps in Libraries in India
2 ; 17 : 51.44'N	Classification of Maps in India in 20th century
234	University Libraries
234'N	20th Century University Libraries

234.44	University Libraries in India
234 : 51	Classification in University Libraries
234 ; 17	Maps in University Libraries
234 ; 17 : 51	Classification of Maps in University Libraries
234 ; 17 : 51'N	Classification of Maps in University Library in 20th century
234 ; 17 : 51.44	Classification of Maps in University Libraries in India
24 (L)	Medical Libraries

To illustrate further, another sequence of class numbers is given below:

YaN9	Bibliography on Sociology brought upto 1990s
Y0b NB	Sociology for Town Planners
Y'M	19th Century Sociology
Y : 4	Social Pathology
Y15	Woman Sociology
Y150w6	Difference between Men and Women Sociology
Y15 : 4	Women Social Pathology
Y15-31	Rural Women Sociology
Y15-31 : 4	Social Pathology of Rural Women

Though the filing process in the CC seems quite a mental ordeal, but with practice it becomes more and more mechanical.

10

CC INDEX

Ranganathan never undermined the need of a good index despite his structured approach to classifying. At the same time, the CC schedules being quite handy and slender, the index in the CC is not indispensable to the extent it is in the DDC. Accordingly a small alphabetical index of the terms given under various main classes and common isolates (CI)s has been given at the end of part second, viz. from pages 2.24 to 2.72.

Scope

Type of index Ranganathan devised is known as a **featured index**. It is one stage advanced than Dewey's Relative Index. Like his scheme, his index too is a different one. It is a thin rather sparse index consisting of 47 pages only. The index to the CC does not aim to be an alphabetical list of all the subjects which could be synthesised according to the scheme. It also does not enlist all those isolates which can be synthesised or sharpened by the use of various devices; nor it provides readymade class numbers. Complex subjects too have not been enumerated. In such an index there is no question of enumerating all the hundred thousands of compound subjects. But the class numbers for compound subjects of first order can be obtained through the index, as the basic class to which an isolate belongs is also given in the index. The index indicates through symbols and abbreviations the main class(es) and the facet(s) to which a given term belongs.

Space Isolates (Chap. 4) and Personality Isolates in I Botany and K Zoology have their separate index each given at the end of their respective schedules. Therefore, for these isolates no effort should be made to locate them through the general index. Similarly classics have their own index given at the end of part three. Thus there are five indexes in addition to one concept index given at the end of part one.

Arrangement

The entries have been arranged in a word by word order following the principle of nothing before something:

Abstract noun
Abstraction
Age proportion
Agency

In case of phrases no set order seems to have been followed. Sometimes a phrase is inverted so as to bring together all the phrases constituent of the same key word, while in other cases phrases have been indexed without inversion, that is given in their natural order. As consequence of such an inconsistent policy some of the terms have been indexed twice:

Acid, Organic; Organic acid.

While some terms such as "Organic Chemistry" have not been indexed at all.

Against every entry the index number consisting of the main or canonical class and the facet to which it belongs along with its isolate number has been given. Various abbreviations used in the index have amply been explained in the beginning of the Index:

Anger R4 [P], 141 S [E] 524

means that the term anger occurs in the first level personality of the canonical class R4 Ethics where its isolate number is 141 : and it also occurs in the energy facet of S Psychology where its isolate number is 524.

Similarly Circulatory system G [P], K[P2], L[P] 3 should be read as that the term circulatory system occurs in the personality of main class G Biology; in the second level personality facet of main class K Zoology and again in the personality of main class L Medicine; and in every case its isolate number is 3 (an example of scheduled mnemonics). The sequence of isolates is in classified order, if it occurs in two or more main classes,

Again :

Criticism (PCEI), g

means that the "Criticism" is posteriorising Common Energy Isolate, and its digit is "g".

Thus one easily gets familiar with these symbols and interprets them as one does the usual alphabets.

As one becomes more and more familiar with the use of the scheme the use of the index is minimised. Moreover, Ranganathan always suggested, rather strongly desired, to follow the hierarchical method in locating an isolate—always getting more and more specific, till one reaches the desired isolate. In his famous steps for practical classification there is no step for the use of the index. But a classifier is never equally at ease in all the disciplines. In some subjects outside one's academic background the classifier may not be knowing the affiliation and location of some isolates. In such circumstances the CC index helps the students and the practitioners as well.

11

SOURCES OF READYMADE CC CLASS NUMBERS

Dr Dahlberg[1] writes about the use of the scheme as follows:

"According to Gopinath, the CC sixth edition has been used in about 2,500 libraries in India, mostly in public libraries, but also in nearly 20 Universities, 200 special and 1,000 college libraries. It is used in classifying articles by some journals in India [e.g., *Herald of Library Science*] and the Indian National Bibliography. It is also used by a small number of libraries in England [e.g. Christ's College Cambridge[2,3]] and Metal Box Ltd. London and in Africa, namely College of Agriculture Library, Khartoum, Sudan.[4] This classification is taught to students at the bachelor and master of library science levels in almost all the Indian universities.[5] It is also taught at lower levels of library education in India.

Therefore, for readymade CC numbers one can look for INB and the accession lists of the libraries using this scheme. *Indian Library Science Abstracts* also uses this scheme for classifying its entries. All such publications are useful sources for providing practical examples of the CC numbers besides Ranganathan's own books such as CCC, the *Library Book Selection*, and *Library Manual* where CC numbers have been given to some books.[6] Part 3 of CC-6 provides readymade class numbers for classics.

REFERENCES

1. Dahlberg, Ingetraut, "Major Developments in Classification" in *Advances in Librarianship*, Vol. 7 (1977), p. 64
2. Maltby, Arthur Sayers' *Manual of Classification for Librarians*, 5th ed., London, Andre Deutsch, 1975, p. 202.
3. Davison, Keith, *Theory of Classification*, Bombay, Asia, 1966, p. 20.

4. Bakewell, K.G.B : Classification and Indexing Practice, London, Clive Bingley, 1978, pp. 94-100.
5. Gopinath, M.A., "Colon Classification" in A. Maltby, ed., *Classification in the 1970's : A Second Look*, Bingley, 1976, pp. 51-80.
6. Satija, M.P. "Use of Colon Classification" *Int Classif* 13 (2), 1986, pp. 88-92.

PART II

PRACTICAL APPLICATIONS

INTRODUCTION

In this part a chapter each has been allotted to every main class recognised by the Colon Classification. These chapters deal particularly with the exceptional rules and peculiarities of each main class. One may wonder as to why to deal with each main class individually when all the rules in general have already been discussed with ample illustrations. The fact is that in the CC every main class abounds with many exceptions or problems peculiar to that main class. These peculiar problems can only be solved by the classifiers by some special methods devised and suggested by Ranganathan; otherwise, there is no solution to them even if one is master of all general rules. In this part solutions of such problems have been explained with sufficient illustrations. Chapters under Part II also contain examples illustrating the use of Common Isolates, Phase Relations, various Devices and parallel schedules. Facet formula of every main class has been discussed in detail and the facets under each category have been explained. Examples have been so chosen so as to drive home the intricacies and finesse of a rule under discussion. This may help the learners to understand such rules not only firmly but also to feel at home with them.

12

z GENERALIA

When every subject is assignable to one and only one main class, then there should be no subject as a truly generalia class. In fact there is no generalia subject; only there are generalia documents—which hold together bits of knowledge from various disparagedly varied subjects. Generalia class is not a mutually exclusive subdivision of knowledge but an adjunct of book classification necessitated by the need of readers. Every subject is so equally present that it is difficult or unjustified to class the document in any of the subject. For example, let us take a daily newspaper, it contains news on large panorama of subjects—social, political, economical, criminal, law, legislature and so on. For such documents, Ranganathan has created a generalia main class z. It contains documents such as universal encyclopaedias, general periodicals, and generalia bibliography. Apart from these, books on area studies, such as Indology, Sinology, Asiana, and multifaceted persons such as Gandhiana, Nehruana, also fall in this class.

The bare digit z may be amplified by (ACI), (AD) and (GD). There is a very queer rule that whenever the bare digit z is amplified by an (ACI) digit, then the digit z should be omitted and the class number should begin with the (ACI) digit only. (Rule 9z4 page 1.62).

Thus a general encyclopaedia will get the class number k, (not zk). General Bibliography will get the class number a (not za); and similarly a general periodical will get the class number m (not zm). The (ACI)s may, of course, be further fitted with their own facets—the facets $[P_1]$ and $[P_2]$ of the (ACI) to be got by (GD) and (CD) respectively.

Encyclopaedia Britannica
k56, L

Encyclopedia Americana
k73, M

The Hindu
m44, M80

Illustrated Weekly of India
m44, M81
Encyclopaedia of World Biography
wk1, N73

In case of a person coming as a class, z may be amplified by (AD)—the name of the person:

zG	Gandhiana
zN	Nehruana
zP	Platoana

Here z is not to be omitted. Designating a person as a class helps to bring together all his/her works belonging to different subjects.

Bibliography on Nehru brought upto 1970s
zNaN7
Gandhian Institute
zG.44, d, 9N36
Journal of Gandhian Studies, 1973+
zGm44, N7

For area studies z may be amplified by (GD).

z44	Indology
z4	Orientology
z41	Sinology

Which may be further amplified.

Bibliography on Sinology brought upto 1985
z41aN9
Indian Journal of American Studies
z73 m44, N
Vishweshvara Vishva Bandhu Institute of Sanskrit and Indological Studies (Hoshiarpur, Punjab)
z44.4443.H, d, V

The schedule of z generalia class with enumerated isolates is "a Generalia Bibliography" and its facet formula is:

$$a[P_1], [P_2] [P_3], [P_4]$$

$[P_1]$ stands for the kind of bibliography—other than textual contents. It includes the material to be included in the bibliography or catalogue. Its isolates have been enumerated. It would be observed in the practical work that a complete isolate will have to be frequently got by the (SID). Too much application of (SID) makes one feel that there is some snag in the coverage of $[P_1]$ isolates:

$[P_2]$ means the issuing authority, viz., whether a bookseller or a publisher.

$[P_3]$ is to be got by (CD) or (AD) depending upto $[P_2]$.

$[P_4]$ also depends upon $[P_2]$ and is got by (CD), if required.

The variation chart for $[P_3]$ and $[P_4]$ has been given at page 1.63. One has to constantly refer to this chart.

Catalogue of the books of the Manager of Publications
a43-55, 3M

M standing for "Manager" is here $[P_3]$ and has to be got by (AD). $[P_3]$ is always got by (AD) if (IN) in $[P_2]$ is 3 or 4. In our case it is 3.

Similarly,

Autumn 2001 catalogue of Periodicals from the Pergamon Press
a46-58, 3P'P01 'n7

Union catalogue of Periodicals in India in 1999
a46, 144, N9

A catalogue of the Exhibition of India's Nineteenth century Manuscripts
a12, 544, M

Reading List of Children Books
a811, 7

Bibliography of Russian Books translated into Punjabi
a95142-153

95 has first been divided by the original language, i.e., 142 Russian, then by the other language. A hyphen separates the two.

Indian Book Review
a43, 144 : gm44.N81

Bibliography of Bibliographies
aa

Biography Index (US, 1946+)
wam73, N4

The subject catalogues and the subject bibliographies must be classed with their respective subjects.

Union Catalogue of Scientific Periodicals in Bengal
Aa46, 14475

Catalogue of Biology books from Cambridge University Press
Ga43, 3C

Indian National Bibliography (INB)
a43, 144n44, N5

13

2 LIBRARY SCIENCE

Facet formula is:

2[P] ; [M] : [E] [2P]

[P] is the kind of library. Its isolates are enumerated, and the (IN) 4 can be further sharpened by (SD).

[M] is the kind of document under process. Its isolates are the same as that of [P] of a Generalia Bibliography.

[E] cum [2P] are library techniques, procedures and processes.

In case of 2 : 51 or its extensions, [2P] is the subject classified and is to be got by (SD) preceded by the digit 9.[1] Though usually between [E] and [2P] no comma is put, but here it is necessary as the number of digits in [E] 51 vary as this can be amplified by (CD).

In case of specific classification systems 2 : 51 may be individualized by (CD) subject to the rules for applying (CD):

Public Libraries in Punjab
22.4443

Classification of Science Books
2 : 51, 9(A)
(Here A Science has been got by SD)

Comparative study of DC and CC
2 : 51M0vN3
(Intra-Array Comparison relation)

Difference in the treatment of Mathematics in UDC and LC classification schemes:
2 : 51M960wN, 9(B)
(Intra-Array Difference Relation)

Classification of Microfilms in Economics in the University Libraries of UK in 1980's
234 ; 1512 : 51, 9(X). 56 'N8

Colon Classification of Microfilms in Economics in the University Libraries of UK in 21st Century
234 ; 1512 : 51N3,9(X).56 'P

National Library of Medicine (USA)
213-4(L).73

Selection of Microfilms in the National Science Library of India
213-4(A) ; 1512 : 1.44

It has not been mentioned explicitly that [2P] in case of other Energy Isolates may also be got by (SD), as we get in the case of [E] 51. But there is nothing to prevent the extension of above rules to any of the other Energy Isolates, 1, 5, 55, 6, 7, 81 and 97. Similarly the cataloguing codes, too, may be individualized by (CD) as in the case of 2 : 51.

Charles C Jewett's Cataloguing code (1852)
2 : 55M5

Cutter's Rule for a printed Dictionary Catalogue (1876)
2 : 55M7

Ranganathan's classified catalogue code (1934)
2 : 55N3

Cataloguing of Literary Manuscripts in Research Libraries
236 ; 12 : 55, 9(O)

Cataloguing of Literary Manuscripts in Research Libraries according to Cutter's Code
236 ; 12 : 55M7, 9(O)

Selection of Science books in University Libraries[2]
234 : 1(A)

Current Awareness Service in Government Department Libraries
248 : 97

Difference of giving reference service in District Public Libraries and College Libraries
2210n33 : 7

Documentation in Chemistry in Science Libraries
24(A) : 97(E)

Encyclopaedia of Library and Information Science (Marcel-Dekker)
2k73, N7

International study conference on classification, Elsinore (1965)
2 : 51p1, N65

A Librarian looks back, Autobiography of Dr. S.R. Ranganathan
2wM92, 1

Collected works of B.I. Palmer (1910-1979)
2xN10

Report of Advisory Committee for Libraries (Chairman, K.P. Sinha)
2.44'N57t

Documentation Research and Training Centre (Bangalore : 1962)
2.44, f, 9N62

Indian Association of Special Libraries and Information Centres, 1955
24.44, g, 9N

Powers of the President of Indian Association of Academic Librarians (INDAAL)
23.44, g, 9N, 1 : 3

Economic powers of the President of INDAAL
23.44, g, 9N, 1 : 3(X)

C'Wealth Library Association
2.1N48, g, 9N72

History of Library Legislation in India brought upto 1970's
2 : (Z)v44 'N7

History of Indian Library Association from 1933 to 2001
2.44, g, 9N3v 'P01 ← N33

Philosophy of Librarianship
2 : (R)

Application of Computers in Book Selection
2 : 81 : (D6, 8(B))

Library Association Record
2m56, M

Library Journal
2m73, M

Inter-lending Review (BL 1972) (A Journal about Inter-Library Cooperation)
2 : 4m56, N
(Supposing that it is the first British Journal on the subject).

Library and Information Science Abstracts, (LISA, London, 1961+)
2am56, N6

International Federation of Library Associations and Institutions (IFLA, 1927)
2.1, d, g, 9N2

International Society for Knowledge Organization (ISKO, 1989, Frankfurt)
2 : 51.1, g, 9N8

Library Association of SAARC (LASAARC, 1992)
2.4N8, g, 9N

REFERENCES

1. See the correction for these examples at page 1.64 in the Annexure page 23.
2. In these cases between [E] and [2P] no comma is necessary according to Rule 0566, page 1.28.

14

B MATHEMATICS

In the CC, the enumeration of isolates in the mathematics schedule is quite exhaustive and indepth. Yet it is quite simple to apply. Statistics, Mechanics, Physico-mathematics and Astronomy have been enumerated as parts of mathematics. Personality occurs in three levels in B33 Differential and Integral equations. Extensive use of (CD) has been made in case of theorems.

At the first instance, mathematics has been divided canonically. Personality and Energy isolates vary from canonical class to canonical class. There is no [M] nor [2E]. [P] is usually the kind, degree or order of the equation and [E] is the solution.

Sixth order ordinary Linear Equations
B331, 1, 6

Differential Plane Geometry
B62 : 3

Non-Euclidean Descriptive Line Geometry
B6M, 1 : 5

Three Dimensional Elliptic Geometry
B6M3, 3

Dynamics of Viscous Liquids
B756 : 3

Lunar Eclipse
B92 : 57

Moon tides in the Indian Ocean
B92 : 78.95

Calculating the Mass of the Earth
B91 : 622 : b1

(b1 is a posteriorising Energy Common Isolate)

Indian Standard Time
B9 : 165.44

Age of the Earth
B91 : 67

Astro-Chemistry
B9 : (E)

Life of John Kepler—the Great Astronomer (1571-1630)
B9wJ71

Collected Astronomical Works of Galileo
B9xJ64

Graphical solutions to Abelian equations
B239M:6

Influence of Tensor Calculus on the Theory of Relativity
CN0g B463

Difference between cardinal and ordinal numbers
B3111ow3

All India Seminar on Probability Theory (Calcutta, 1975)
B281p44, N75

Journal of the Indian Mathematical Society (1937+)
Bm44, N3

Nizamiah (National) Observatory (Hyderabad)
B9.44, f2, N

Mensuration
B6 : (B1)

Occult Arithmetic
Δ (B1)

Indian Institute of Astrophysics (Bangalore, 1972)
B9 : 6.44, d, 9N

International Mathematical Union (Paris, 1952)
B.1, g, 9N5

15

C PHYSICS

Like mathematics, physics, too, has, at the first instance, been divided into canonical classes. Systems and specials of physics have been given at the end of the physics schedule, as usual. Matter is usually not present, but as per 4th example at page 1.71 it may be got by Mnemonic Device. Similarly, it may also be got by (SD) if necessary:

Pressure of Gases
C28 : 7[1]

Michelson Morley Experiment on the Velocity of Light (1887)
C51 : 21 M87

(Since it was a classic experiment on the velocity of light, so has been treated like a system)

Fizeau Method for determining the Velocity of light (1849)
C51 : 21M49

Propagation of Sound through metals
C3 : 2; (E191)

It seems that the isolate number under C1 Fundamentals have been misprinted. The correct order seems to be:

C11 Matter
C12 Weight
C13 Gravitation
C14 Energy
C15 Space
C16 Time

Melting point of organic substances
C4; (E5) : 512

Fluid Theory of Heat (Put forth in the 18th century)
C4 : 8L

Joule's Theory of Heat (1850)
C4 : 8M5

Nuclear Fission
C9B3 : 11

Neutron Spectroscopy
C9B31 : 3

Nature of Light according to Relativity Theory
CN, 51 : 8

Space and Time according to Gravitation Theory
CK, 81

Low Temperature Wave Mechanics
CN2, 9D1

Elasticity of Glass at High Temperatures
C9D8, 215 : 2

Diffusion of Gases at Low temperature according to Wave Mechanics
CN2, 9D1, 28 : 93

A Comparative study of the Corpuscular and Quantum Theories of Light
C51 : 8KowN

Life of J.J. Thomson (1856-1940)
CwM56

Physics Papers of Sir Isaac Newton (1642-1727)
CxK42

An Occult Conception of Einstein's Theory of Relativity
Δ (CN)

Practical Physics
C : f3

Saha Institute of Nuclear Physics (Calcutta, 1951)
C9B3.44, d, S

International Commission on Illumination (1900)
C5 : 28.1'N00t5

Mass Energy Relation
C830t4

Mathematical Equation of Mass and Energy
C830t4 : (B)

Mathematical Physics
C : (B)

Indian Journal of Pure and Applied Physics (1963+)
Cm44, N6

REFERENCE

1. In the schedule of C2 Properties of Matter isolates enumerated as [P2] are actually Energy Isolates. Misprint may be corrected.

16

D ENGINEERING

Engineering is a very vast discipline having many branches in its fold. Ranganathan implicitly takes Engineering only as a sort of applied physics—a very narrow definition. Modern branches of Engineering have either altogether been omitted or their enumeration is scanty. The main classes allied to D Engineering are F Technology, HZ Mining and M useful Arts—these are supplements to it.

The first division of Engineering is on canonical basis. Though each canonical class has its own personality isolates, even then a common connective of all the Personality Isolates can be found out:

[P] is the kind of work

$[P_2]$ is the part of work, so it varies according to [P]—meaning that $[P_2]$ isolates are not common for all isolates of $[P_1]$.[1] However for D6 Mechanical Engineering $[P_2]$ means the field of applications. Its isolates, if not enumerated, may be got by (SD).

$[P_3]$ is part of work of D6. Its isolates have not been enumerated in this schedule. Perhaps, these would be enumerated in the depth version of the schedule.[2]

[E] cum [2P] are various engineering operations.

D66 Electrical Engineering has some Common Isolates specially meant for it. Its isolates have been enumerated at the end of the schedule viz., page 2.45.

Constructing Brick Roofs
D33, 6 : 7

Surveying for underground Railway Platform
D4154, 87 : 2

Specifications for the floor of Dining Cars in Rail Carriages
D515335, 63 : 5

Tram Car Roof Repair
D5151, 66 : 85

Aerial Survey for Airport site
D43, 8 : 28
Machine Tools
D6, 8
Drilling Tools
D6, 845
Repair of Harvesting Machinery
D6, 8(J : 7) : 85
Dairy Machinery
D6, 8(KZ311 : 71)
Mining Equipment
D6, 8(HZ)
Design of Nuclear Reactors in India
D7, 13 : 4.44

As mentioned in the schedule and also from the hierarchical principle, we can infer that all the isolates of [P_2] for D6 are also equally valid for all its branches, i.e., all parts of D6:

Mechanical Lifts
D6, 71
Electrical Lifts
D66, 71
Hydraulic Lifts
D635, 71
Mechanical Printers
D6, 8(M14)
Electronic Printers
D65, 8(M14)
Electronic Clocks
D65, 8(B9 : 165)
Maintenance of Electronic Translating Machines
D65, 8(P : 795) : 82
Designing Electronic Computers
D65, 8(B) : 4
Storage of Weak Current
D665, 18
Maintenance of Underground Electrical Transmission Lines
D66, 24 : 82
Alternating Current (AC) Meter
D664e3
Energy meters for overhead transmission of Two Phase AC
D6642, 21e5

Purification of (Water Supply) water by Salts
D85534

The last digit 4 has been got from E Chemistry as per instructions under D8553.

Chlorination of Drinking Water
D8553171

Difference between the generation of AC and DC Currents
D6630w4 : 1

Influence of Electrical Engineering on Civil Engineering
D1 or 66

Institution of Engineers Bulletin (1951+)
Dm44, N5

All India Annual Conference of Electrical Engineers (2001, New Delhi)
D66p44, P01

Bulletin of Electronic Society of India (1970)
D65m44, N7

Guru Nanak Engineering College, Ludhiana
D.4443, e4, G

Functions of the Institute of Engineers India (1920)
D.44, d, 9N : 3

REFERENCES

1. It is known as Differential Facet. (See Chapter 8).
2. Please note in the D Engineering Schedule (page 2.40) the facet formula is wrongly printed as D[P], [2P][P_2] : [E]. It should be corrected to D[P], [P_2] : [E] [2P].

17

E CHEMISTRY

A preeminent branch of physical sciences, the Chemistry has for its object of study the structure and composition of substances. Commensurate with the breadth and depth of the subject, Ranganathan tried to be quite thorough in enumerating isolates for E Chemistry. But this most dynamic of the physical sciences foils all man-made attempts to contain it by such extrinsic methods. In the CC, though not stated explicitly, the main class E Chemistry has been divided into canonical branches: Inorganic Chemistry and Organic Chemistry. Physical Chemistry and Analytical Chemistry occur appropriately in Energy Isolates—yes, they are all action. Elaborate rules have also been provided for constructing class numbers for inorganic compounds such as hydroxides, oxides, acids, bases and salts. Rules for constructing isolate numbers for organic substances and their derivatives are comparatively simple. But as said earlier, these rules are quite inadequate to individualize nearly infinite chemical compounds, both organic and inorganic. Rules only result in almost primitive grouping of chemicals. Many new branches find no mention in the schedules or have not been accorded a due status as per their literary warrant. These broad grouping has resulted in many homonymous isolate numbers: many different chemical compounds get the same isolate number. Many kinds of compounds and the recently discovered elements (with atomic number more than 100) have not been included in elements—though their substance number can be constructed as per the rules given. A special index for chemical substance especially elements would have been quite useful. Some misprints and anomalies in rules and isolates have also been pointed out.[1] The facet formula is: E[P], $[P_2]$: [E][2P], $[2P_2]$.

[P] : elements or compounds, organic and inorganic, collectively termed as substance number.

$[P_2]$: organic derivatives, so applies differentially to E 5, E 6, E 7 and E 8.

[E] cum [2P] : Chemical processes and manipulations.

[$2P_2$] : Analytical methods and techniques. This facet is differential for E : 3.

Inorganic Substances

E 1 to E 4 are all branches of Inorganic Chemistry, so it is a telescoped array. E1 deals with the chemical elements; and E2 to E4 deal with various Inorganic compounds. But there is no isolate number for all the inorganic substances taken together. In case of E1 elaborate rules exist for constructing isolate number of chemical elements. In the CC the classification of elements is based on the Periodic Table. But the problem is that the periodic table itself is not without anomalies. An Isolate Number for an element usually consists of three digits and in some cases of five digits also. In a substance number of an element the first digit 1 stands for the substance element, the second digit for the group to which it belongs in the periodic table, and the third digit is its period number in the periodic table. For example, the isolate number 182 for Iron may be analysed: first digit 1 stands for the element, the second digit 8 stands for the eighth group in the periodic table, and the third digit 2 stands for the period of iron in the periodic table. If more than three digits occur in an isolate number of an element, the extra digits are only to accommodate the element in the already pre-occupied cell of the periodic table. Since (IN)s for almost all the known elements (with the exception of a few unstable elements) have been enumerated, so the rules from E1 to E119 (page 1.74) only explain the rationale behind assigning (IN)s to the Chemical elements. They may, however, be used to fix the isolate numbers for the chemical elements, which have not been enumerated in the CC or may be discovered in the future. On the basis of these rules the possible substance number for the following elements are given below:

Einsteinium	(Es)	13791
Fermium	(Fr)	13792
Mendelevium	(Md)	13793
Nobelium	(No)	13794
Lawrencium	(Lr)	13795
Rutherfordium	(Rf)	1479
Hahnium	(Ha)	1579

Before constructing class numbers for inorganic compounds, it is a prerequisite to understand the term "**Element Number**" and "**Full Element Number**":

Element Number is defined by Ranganathan as the group of digits following the digit 1 in E1 (Rule E111 page 1.74). In other words the element number usually consists of the group number followed by the period number in periodic table. It may be noted that only the elements can have any element number, not the compounds. For example, the element number for Hydrogen is 10, for Zinc it is 23 and for Helium it is 00, for Platinum it is 879 and for Actinium it is 391, and so on.

For Full Element Number the Valency Number is added to the Element Number.

Full Element Number=Element Number+Valency Number

For example, the Full Element Number for Hydrogen is 10+1=101. Similarly, the full element number for Zinc is 23+2=232, for Helium it is 00+0=000 and for Actinium it is 391+3=3913.

It may be noted that some of the elements exhibit more than one valency number depending upon the compound. Platinum has two valency numbers 3 or 4; Gold has valency 1 or 3. Similarly Chromium has three valency numbers 2, 3 or 6. And various valency numbers for Manganese (Mn) are 2, 3, 4, 6 and 7. Therefore, the full Element Number of these elements also vary from compound to compound. The Full Element Numbers of the above elements are as follows, for example:

Platinum	(Pt)	8793 or 8794
Gold	(Au)	181 or 183
Chromium	(Cr)	622, 623, 626
Manganese	(Mn)	722, 723, 724, 726 and 727

Hydroxides

Substance number for a hydroxide is got by adding to the digit 2 the Element Number of the element whose hydroxide is under study, viz., the Basic element. For example, water which has been treated as hydrogen Hydroxide [(H(OH)] for this purpose will get the substance number:

2+10=210

Similarly the substance number for sodium hydroxide Na(OH) (Caustic soda) is:

2+11=211

Substance number for some of the hydroxides are given below:

Potassium hydroxide	KOH	212
Calcium hydroxide	$Ca(OH)_2$	222
Aluminium hydroxide	$Al(OH)_3$	231
Iron hydroxide	Fe(OH)	282

Oxides

For *Oxides*, the Full Element Number of the element whose oxides is the primary focus should be added to the digit 2. The formula is:

2+Element Number+Valency *or* 2+Full Element Number

For example, substance number of Ferrous Oxide: FeO is

2+82+2=2822

Similarly, substance number for some of the oxides are given below:

Ferric oxide	Fe_2O_3	2+82+3=2823
Sodium oxide	Na_2O	2+11+1=2111
Lead Monoxide	PbO	2+48+2=2482
Carbon dioxide	CO_2	2+40+4=2404
Manganese dioxide	MnO_2	2+72+4=2724

Acids

For Acids the substance number is constructed by adding to the digit 3 the Full Element Number of the constituent elements. Let us make the substance number for sulphuric acid H_2SO_4. Here sulphur is the element whose oxide forms the acid. Element number for sulphur is 61 and valency number is 6 in this case. Thus the Full Element Number for sulphur is 616. Hence the substance number for sulphuric acid is 3+616=3616. Similarly, the Substance Number for other acids are:

Nitric Acid	HNO_3	3505
Hydrochloric Acid	HCl	3711
Hydrofloric Acid	HF	3701
Hydrobromic Acid	HBr	3731

Salts

For Salts, as per 9th example on page 1.76, the substance number is got by adding to 4 the Element Numbers for basic and acidic elements respectively. For example, the substance number for Sodium Chloride NaCl:

4+Element Number of Sodium+Element Number of Chlorine=4+11+71=41171

Substance number for Gold Chloride AuCl:
4+18+71–41871

Similarly:

Silver Bromide AgBr =41573

Zinc Sulphide ZnS =4+23+61=42361
Barium Chloride BaCl =4+26+71=42671

Similarly the substance number for Potassium chloride KCl is = 41271

The substance numbers for some of the salts are given below:

Gold Chloride	41871
Sodium Bromide	41173

In case of Organic and Biochemical substances, the substance Number exists in two levels. [P_2] called the combination number enumerates the derivatives of organic and biochemical substances. This provides individualization only upto the family level, not upto the individual member. For example, both the Methyl chloride CH_3Cl and Methyl Bromide CH_3Br have the same class Numbers E611, 1. This nevertheless provides great hospitality.

Class Numbers for some of the Organic or Biochemical substances and their derivatives are given below:

Aliphatic Sulfuric Acid (It is a sulphur Compound of an aliphatic substance)
E6, 6

(Laboratory)Preparation of Methyl chloride
E611, 1 : 11

Solubility of Ethyl Bromide
E612, 1 : 2201

Aliphatic Silicons
E6, 841

(Here 8 of [P_2] has been amplified by the Element Number of the Silicon as per Rule E28, page 1.76).

Synthesis of Aromatic Esters
E7, 383 : 4

Benzoic Acid (Acid of Benzene)
E711, 3

Aniline (Amino Benzene)
E711, 51

Dimethyl Ether
E611, 281

Dehydration of Methanethoil
E611, 6 : 82

Nitromethane
E611, 57

(The isolate number 7 in [P_2] (page 2.48) for Nitro compounds seems to be a misprint. The correct isolate number appears to be 57 instead of 7).

Commercial Quantitative Analysis of Acetic Acid
E612, 3 : 34, 6

Difference between the preparation of Ethers and Ketones
E5, 2810w5 : 11

Biochemistry of Vitamins
E9G, 97

Quantitative analysis of Proteins by Raman Spectra in Biochemistry
E9G, 92Z2 : 33, E7

Organic Physical Chemistry
E5 : 2

Some Examples from Inorganic Chemistry

Periodic Table of Chemical Elements
E1 : 17

This can further be sharpened by (CD) in case of various periodic systems.

Mendeleyev's Periodic Table (1869)
E1 : 17M6

Thomsen's Periodic Table (1895)
E1 : 17M9

Difference between Atomic weights of oxygen and sulphur
E160 0w1 : 14

Oxidation of Sulphur
E161 : 81

pH value of Salts
E4 : 3, T6

Qualitative analysis of water by Electrical Method
E210 : 33, F

Valency of Radium
E129 : 215

Synthesis of Nitric Acid
E3505 : 4

Influence of Physical Chemistry on Inorganic Chemistry
E10gE : 2

Relation between organic and inorganic chemistry
E10j5

Indian Chemical Society (1924)
E.44, g, 9N

Indian Institute of Metals (Calcutta, 1946)
E191.44, d, 9N

Society of Biological Chemists (India, 1930)
E9G. 44, g, 9N

International Union of Pure and Applied Chemistry (IUPAC) (Oxford 1919)
E.1, g, 9N1

Biography of Sir Humphry Davy (1778-1829)
EwL78

Chemical Abstracts
Eam73, M

Russian Journal of Physical Chemistry
E : 2m47, N

Indian Journal of Chemistry (1963+)
Em44, N6

Estimating the quantity of Sulphur in Sulphuric Acid
E36160k161 : 34
(See Rule E18, page 1.76)

Determining the presence of Copper in an alloy by Electrical Method
E1930k13 : 33, F

Bibliography of Chemical Physics 1995
E : (C)aN9

History of Indian Chemistry brought upto 2000AD
Ev44 'P1

REFERENCE

1. Arora, G.K., *et al.* "Classification of Chemical Compounds in CC : Inorganic Compounds 1" *Annals of Lib. Sc. and DoC*, 11 (4), Dec. 1964, pp. 47-53.

APPENDIX TO E CHEMISTRY

Symbol	Name of the Element	Substance Number	Element Number	Valence Number	Full Element Number
(1)	(2)	(3)	(4)	(5)	(6)
Ac	Actinium	1391	391	3	3913
Ag	Silver (Argentum)	115	15	1	151
Al	Aluminium	131	31	3	313
Am	Americium	1694	694	—	—
Ar	Argon	102	02	0	020
As	Arsenic	153	53	3 or 5	533, 535
At	Astatine	178	78	—	—
Au	Gold (Aurum)	118	18	1 or 3	181, 183
B	Boron	130	30	3	303
Ba	Barium	126	26	2	262
Be	Beryllium (glucinium)	120	20	2	202
Bi	Bismuth	158	58	3 or 5	583, 585
Bk	Berkelium	1696	696	—	—
Br	Bromine	173	73	1 or 7	731, 737
C	Carbon	140	40	4	404
Ca	Calcium	122	22	2	222
Cd	Cadmium	125	25	1 or 2	251, 252
Ce	Cerium	146	46	3 or 4	463, 464
Cf	Californium	1697	697	—	—
Cl	Chlorine	171	71	1, 3, 5, 7	711, 713, 715, 717
Cm	Curium	1695	695	—	—
Co	Cobalt	183	83	2 or 3	832, 833
Cr	Chromium	162	62	2, 3 or 6	622, 623, 626
Cs	Caesium	116	16	1	161

(Contd.)

Appendix to E Chemistry (*Contd.*)

(1)	(2)	(3)	(4)	(5)	(6)
Cu	Copper (cuprum)	113	13	1 or 2	131, 132
Dy	Dysprosium	117	17	3	173
Er	Erbium	127	27	3	273
Es	Einsteinium	—	—	—	—
Eu	Europium	167	67	2 or 3	672, 673
F	Fluorine	170	70	1	701
Fe	Iron (ferrum)	182	82	2 or 3	822, 823
Em	Ferium	—	—	—	—
Fr	Francium	1191	191	—	—
Ga	Gallium	133	33	3	333
Gd	Gadolinium	176	76	3	763
Ge	Germanium	143	43	4	434
Hx	Hydrogen	110	10	1	101
Ha	Hahnium	—	—	—	—
He	Helium	100	00	0	000
Hf	Hafnium	147	47	4	474
Hg	Mercury (hydrargyrum)	128	28	1 or 2	281, 282
Ho	Holmium	1179	179	3	1793
I	Iodine	175	75	1, 3, 5, 7	751, 753, 755, 757
In	Indium	135	35	3	353
Ir	Iridium	188	88	2 or 4	882, 884
K	Potassium (kalium)	112	12	1	121
Kr	Krypton	104	04	0	040
La	Lanthanum	136	36	3	363
Li	Lithium	1109	109	1	1091
Lu	Lutertium	1379	379	3	3793
Lr	Lawrencium	—	—	—	—

(*Contd.*)

Appendix to E Chemistry (*Contd.*)

(1)	(2)	(3)	(4)	(5)	(6)
Md	Mendelevium	—	—	—	—
Mg	Magnesium	121	21	2	212
Mn	Maganese	172	72	2, 3, 4, 6, 7	722, 723, 724, 726, 727
Mo	Molybdenum	164	64	2 or 6	642, 646
N	Nitrogen	150	50	3 or 5	503, 505
Na	Sodium (natrium)	111	11	1	111
Nb	Niobium (columbium)	154	54	5	545
Nd	Neodymium	156	56	3 or 4	563, 564
Ne	Neon	101	01	0	010
Ni	Nickel	1829	829	2 or 3	8292, 8293
No	Nobelium	—	—	—	—
Np	Neptunium	1692	692	—	—
O	Oxygen	160	60	2 or 4	602, 604
Os	Osmium	187	87	2 or 8	872, 878
P	Phosphorus	151	51	3 or 5	513, 515
Pa	Protactinium	159	59	5	595
Pb	Lead (plumbum)	148	48	2 or 4	482, 484
Pd	Palladium	1849	849	2 or 4	8492, 8494
Pm	Promethium (illinium)	1392	392	—	—
Po	Polonium	168	68	2, 3 or 4	682, 683, 684
Pr	Praseodymium	1469	469	3 or 4	4693, 4694
Pt	Platinum	1879	879	3 or 4	8793, 8794
Pu	Plutonium	1693	693	—	—
Ra	Radium	129	29	2	292
Rb	Rubidium	114	14	1	141
Re	Rhenium	177	77	2, 3, 4, 6, 7	772, 773, 774, 776, 777
Rf	Rutherfordium (kurchatovium)	—	—	—	—

(*Contd.*)

Appendix to E Chemistry (*Contd.*)

(1)	(2)	(3)	(4)	(5)	(6)
Rh	Rhodium	185	85	2 or 3	852, 853
Rn	Radon (niton)	109	09	0	090
Ru	Ruthenium	184	84	3, 4, or 8	843, 844, 848
S	Sulphur	161	61	2, 4 or 6	612, 614, 616
Sb	Antimony (stibium)	155	55	3 or 5	553, 555
Sc	Scandium	132	32	3	323
Se	Selenium	163	63	2, 4 or 6	632, 634, 636
Si	Silicon	141	41	4	414
Sm	Samarium	166	66	3	663
Sh	Tin (stannum)	145	45	2 or 4	452, 454
Sr	Strontium	124	24	2	242
Ta	Tantalum	157	57	5	575
Tb	Terbium	1769	769	3	7693
Tc	Technetium (masurium)	174	74	—	—
Te	Tellurim	165	65	2, 4 or 6	652, 654, 656
Th	Thorium	149	49	4	494
Ti	Titanium	142	42	3 or 4	423, 424
Tl	Thalium	138	38	1 or 3	381, 383
Tm	Thulium	1279	279	3	2793
U	Uranium	1691	691	2 or 6	6912, 6916
V	Vandium	152	52	5	525
W	Tungsten (wolfram)	167	67	4 or 6	674, 676
Xe	Xenon	106	06	0	060
Y	Yttrium	134	34	3	343
Yb	Ytterbium	137	37	3	373
Zn	Zinc	123	23	2	232
Zr	Zirconium	144	44	4	444

18

F TECHNOLOGY

In the CC, the term "Technology" has been used very confusingly. Ranganathan has restricted the scope of the (MC) F Technology only to Chemical Technology or Industrial Chemistry, meaning the mass or industrial production of Chemicals and their byproducts. It also includes Food and Feul Technology. Enumeration of isolates, especially in the problem facet is toc scanty.

[P] : It is the substance facet. Its isolates are the same as the [P] of E Chemistry in addition to some enumerated isolates.

[E] cum [2P] means the problem facet as well as the process facet. Isolates for the problem facet have to be taken from E Chemistry. The digits following 8 in E : 8 are to be taken as the problem. (Rule F22 page 1.77)

Fermentation of Alcohol
F54 : 7
(Here [E] 7 has been taken from E : 87 Chemical Fermentation)

Industrial Chemistry
F

Industrial Oxidation
F : 1

There may be various industrial processes for a single problem. For example, (Hypothetical) ABC process of water distillation, XYZ process of water distillation. Here distillation is the problem and ABC and XYZ are two different processes. In such cases process facet will come earlier followed by the problem facet. *The process and the problem facets are to be separated by a Colon*. The isolates in the process facet are to be got by (AD). And the isolates in the problem facet are the digits following 8 in the energy isolate of E Chemistry. (Rule F23, page 1.78).

ABC Process of Water Distillation
F210 : A : 35

XYZ Process of Water Distillation
F210 : X : 35

Lead-Chamber process of Sulphuric Acid
F3616 : L

According to Rule F2, page 1.77, the process isolate has been got by (AD).

Contact Process of Sulphuric Acid
F3616 : C

Industrial dehydration of Methyl Ether
F611, 281 : 2

Haber process for Ammonia
F1129 : H

Industrial Distillation of Nitro Paraffins
F61, 5 : 35

If there exist more than one industrial forms of a substance, then the isolate number for each form should be got by the Favoured Category Device. Coal is usually graded as follows, so we can assign isolate number accordingly.

High-volatile	A bituminous	551
Medium-volatile	bituminous	5511
Low-volatile	bituminous	5512
Semianthracite		5513
Anthracite		5514

Similar example for iron has been given at page 1.77 (of CC-6).

Difference between Paints and Tanning Material
F58950w7

Difference between the Industrial Colouring of Paints and Tanning Material
F58950w7 : 95

Kirk-Othmer Encyclopaedia of Chemical Technology (1947)
Fk73, N4

Statistics of Soap making units in Punjab in 1960
F9496.4443 'N60s
(Deeming it a stray report)

Report of Shri Ram Chemicals Limited India
F.44, h, Sr

Central Food Technological Research Institute, Mysore (Bangalore, 1950)
F53.44, f, 9N5

Management Board of the Dalmia Biscuit Factory (Rajpura, Punjab)
F53.4443, k, D, 2

Collected works of Louis Pasteur on Alcohol Fermentation
F54 : 7xM22

Indian Arms and Explosive acts
F5594 : (Z44)

Dehydration of Coffee beans
F53 (J481) : 2

Journal of the Colour Society (India, 1962+)
F58m44, N6

Fuel Abstracts and Current Titles (U.K., 1960+)
F55am56, N6

Atlas of Drug Industries in India, 2002
F56fP1.44

19

G BIOLOGY

It is a generic class for life sciences save L Medicine.

[P] is the kind of life.

[E] cum [2P] is the biological problem of life.

The schedule is too simple but the following two special reminders may be borne in mind.

(1) [2M] may be required in case of Energy isolates 33, 341, 345 and 346.

Here the [2M] is the same as the [P] of E Chemistry ; if further required the isolates in [2M] may be got by (SD) :

Chemical effect of nitrogen on tissues
G12 : 33E ; 150

Chemical effect of drugs on tissues
G12 : 33E ; (F56)

(2) The second point of care is that in case of Energy isolates from 12 to 18 and 5 space isolate should be added immediately—without it the subject may appear meaningless or incomplete. The subjects of Fauna, Flora and Ecology are best studied in context of some geographical area.

These two peculiar points are also valid in I Botany, K Zoology, KZ Animal Husbandry, and L Medicine.

Fauna and Flora of India
G : 12.44

Ecology of Indian Ocean
G : 5.95

Nucleus Microphotography
G113 : 1995

British Journal of Indian Fauna and Flora (started in 1962; a hypothetical case)
G : 12.44 m56, N6

(Indian) Journal of Indian Fauna and Flora started in 19th century
G : 12.44mM

In this peculiar example $[P_1]$ to the (ACI) m has not been added, as the space has already been represented in the subject proper. In such cases (as per the first example on page 1.79) where $[P_1]$ of any (ACI) is absent then $[P_2]$ may be added directly without a comma. From this example it is inferred that $[P_1]$ and $[P_2]$ of (ACI) are telescoped as in the case of V : 19 $[P_1]$, $[P_2]$. In these cases if $[P_1]$ is absent $[P_1]$ is added without the use of a comma.

Marine Ecology of Pacific Ocean
G9555 : 5.97

International Seminar on Indian Natural Environments (New Delhi, 1978)
G : 55.44 p1, N78

Virus diseases of Plants and Animals
G : 423

Bengal Natural History Society (Darjeeling, 1923)
G : 12.4475, g, 9N23

Indian Biophysical Society Report (Founded in 1965)
G : (C).44, g, 9N65r

Opium Katabolism
G : 332 ; (J471)

Tobacco Anabolism in Embryo
G9B : 331 ; (J452)

Physical effects of Fasting
G : 346C

Physical effects of Fasting on the Embryo Cells
G9B, 11 : 346C

Tissue Structure
G12 : 2

Forest conservation
G95124 : 527

Theory of Evolution of Life
G : 66

Since there exists many theories of evolution, so these may be treated as systems. Hence G : 66 may be sharpened by (CD), wherever necessary.

Biblical Account of Evolution
G : 66B

Empedocles ideas of Evolution (450BC)
G : 66C

Darwin's theory of Evolution
G : 66M
(or simply G : 66 keeping in view the literary warrant on it)

Genetic effect of X-ray
G : 60gC53

Morphological Differences between Cells and Tissues
G110w2 : 2

Relation between Anatomy and Physiology
G : 20j3

Life of Charles Darwin (Born in 1809)
GwM09

Biological Abstracts (US, 1927+)
Gam73, N

Tropical Environment
G9H : 55

On the analogy of L9H Tropical Medicine, we can make G9H as specials in Biology, meaning, Tropical Biology.

International Society for Tropical Ecology (Varanasi, 1960)
G9H : 5.1, g, 9N6

Tropical Animal Sociology
G9H : 56

Tropical Forests Conservation in Asia
G9H, 95124 : 527.4

Journal of Marine Biology Association of India 1959
G9555m44, N5

Advances in Microbiology research in India brought up to 2000 AD
G91 : fv44 'P1

Indian Institute of Chemical Biology (Calcutta, 1935)
G : (E).44, g, 9N3

20

H GEOLOGY

In the CC, Geology has been divided into eight canonical classes. The schedule is simple and apparently there seems no difficulty. But H6 Palentology has some peculiar rules.

[P], and [E] cum [2P] vary according to the canonical class. Generally [P] is the substance or kind of earth surface; and [E] cum [2P] is the Geological action, process and problem.

In case of H1 Minerology [P] is the same as [P] of E Chemistry. In this canonical class, all the precious stones have been collected under the personality (IN) 9. Thus the class number for precious stones is H19. Isolates in energy have been enumerated.

Classification of Zinc minerals
H1123 : 11

Occurrence of Sulphur in India
H1161 : 155.44

Artificial Production of Pearls in Japan
H198 : 164.42

Genesis of Volcanic Rocks
H211 : 16

Occurrence of Sedimentary Rocks in China
H23 : 155.41

Description of Indian Metamorphic Rocks
H22 : 13.44

Geysers in Himachal
H412.4445

Quaternary stratigraphy of the Himalayas
H55.4.g7H

As said earlier one has to be careful in H6 Paleontology. Firstly here in H6, books only on Paleozoology are to be classed. Therefore, [P] of H6 is the same as [P] of K Zoology. Books on Paleobotany go to I

Botany. As is quite evident in Paleontology time facet is always necessary. **But the isolate numbers for Time are not to be taken from the general schedule of Time isolates**. But it is to be taken from the H5 stratigraphy by replacing H5 by A. It means:

H5 = A
H51 = A1 and so on.

It is necessary because the geological time is not measured in centuries or millennium. These are too small units for evolutionary processes. Time here takes astronomical magnitude. A century or even a millennium is just a pulse beat time for such evolutionary changes:

Mesozoic Age
A3

Recent Times
A55

Paleozoic Hydrozoa
H641 'A2

(Here Paleozoic is the Time, to be taken from H5 and Hydrozoa is a zoological species, to be taken from the personality of K Zoology).

Cainozoic Insects
H686 'A4

Permian Carnivora
H69791 'A26

Fossils of Recent Primates
H6 9797 'A55

Canozoic Aves
H696 'A4

Silurian Protozoa
H62 'A23

Underground deposits of economic value are collected under H7 Economic Geology. [P] and [E] of H7 are the same as that of H1 Minerology.

Salt Deposits of Pakistan
H74.44Q7

Here H7 has been amplified by the digit 4 taken from the personality of E Chemistry, where it means salts:

Hidden Wealth of the Earth in India
H7.44

Underground water in Ganges Delta
H7210.44.e5G

Genesis of Iron Deposits in Bihar
H7182 : 16.4473

Popular Description of Gold Mines in South Africa
H7118 : 13.63

Diamond Deposits in Muslim countries
H791.1(Q7)

Difference in the Genesis of Ruby and Sapphire
H19210w2 : 16

Stratigraphy for Geographers
H5 0bU

Geophysics
H : (C)

Nuclear Geophysics
H : (C9B3)

Mathematical Geophysics
H : (C) : (B)

British Journal of Mathematical Geophysics
H : (C) : (B) m56, N

Geological Survey of India (1851)
H.44, f2, 9M

Central Seismological Observatory
H4132.44, f2, 9N

Journal of Petrology (UK, 1960+)
H2m56, N6

Biblical Account of the Origin of the Earth
H8B

Lord Kelvin's Theory about the Age of Earth (1899)
H8M9

In these cases H8 has been sharpened by (CD) to treat various theories as systems.

21

HZ MINING

It is applied minerology—the large scale economic process of digging ores from the mines and the subsequent process of separating the required mineral from its impurities.

[P] is the ore. This forms the substance facet and is to be taken from the [P] of E Chemistry. Usually an ore contains many substances; the [P] should be the substance which can be extracted economically from it.

[P_2] is the part of the work.

[E] cum [2P] forms the processes involved in mining.

Lighting the underground roads of Iron Mines in Bihar
HZ182, 4 : 55.4473

Surface transport in Sulphur Mines
HZ161, 8

Copper Pits
HZ113, 1

Timbering the Tunnels of Lead Mines
HZ148, 3 : 18

Transactions of the Society of Mining Engineers (USA 1962+)
HZm73, N6

Society of Mining Engineers (USA)
HZ.73, g, 9N

Report of the Indian School of Mining (1926, Dhanbad)
HZ.44, e4, 9N2r

Director of the Central Mining Research Station, Dhanbad (Founded 1956)
HZ.44, f, 9N56, 1

Safety in Mines Abstracts (UK 1952+)
HZ : 4am56, N5

It is one of the drawbacks of this schedule that Metallurgy has been separated from mining. Again no clear cut isolates appear from mining of Coal and Petroleum and other fuel gases.

22

I BOTANY

A sovereign branch of G Biology, it has plants and vegetative life for its objects of study.

[P] is the kind of plant, the natural group. Enumeration is based on the scientific principles of plant taxonomy.

[P_2] is the part (organ) of the plant. Its isolates have been enumerated, and if further required, isolates may be borrowed from the [P] of L Medicine.

[E] cum [2P] denotes the life processes. Its isolates are the same as that the [E] cum [2P] of G Biology. Not only this, G Biology, I Botany, K Zoology and to a large extent L Medicine have a common energy schedule. Paleobotany is an additional energy isolate of I Botany.

In a nutshell I Botany is one of the simple schedules. A special index to the natural groups, i.e., the Personality Isolates has been provided immediately after the schedule on pages 2.61 to 2.63. It is very useful for classifiers not familiar with botanical names of plants. It may be reminded that the two peculiarities of G Biology are equally valid here:

Journal of Indian Flora (Calcutta, 1960+ : a hypothetical case)
I : 13.44mN

British Journal of European Plants (1970+)
I : 13.5m56, N

Chemical effect of Sulphur on Plant Tissues
I, 12 : 33E ; 161

Nitrogen Metabolism in Plants
I : 33 ; 150

Plant Classification (Taxonomy)
I : 11

Since there exist various systems of Plant Classification, so these may be treated as Systems; and the various systems may be got (CD):

John Ray's System of Plant Classification (Propounded in 1660)
I : 11K

Linnaeus System of Plant Classification (formulated in the 18th century)
I : 11L

Hooker-Bentham Plant Classification
I : 11N

Tissues of dicotyledons
I8, 12

Premulales leaf morphology
I845, 15 : 2

Fungi nomenclature
I23 : 11

Himalayan Flora
I : 13.4.g7H

International Conference on Himalayan Flora (New Delhi, 1979)
I : 13.4.g7Hp1, N79

Dictionary of Plant Ecology
I : 5k

Development of Thallophyts
I2 : 7

Reproduction in Flowering Plants
I5 : 67

Microscopic Botany
I : 19

Bark of Daphnales
I885, 87

[Bark may be taken as the skin of the plants. Therefore [P_2] 87 has been borrowed from the [P] of L Medicine. This is in accordance with the instructions given under [P_2] of the Botany Schedule at page 2.60).

Nervous system of Plants
I, 7

Paleobotany
I : 8

Cainozoic Rosales Fossils
I831 : 8 'A4

(Here Time Isolate has been got in the same way as we got in H6 Palaeontology, i.e., by replacing H5 by A).

Fossils of Recent Bryophyta
I3 : 8 'A55

Cretaceous Fossils of the leaves of Pteridophyta
I4, 15 : 8 'A34

Botanica (Journal of Botany, India, 1950)
Im44, N5

Bulletin of the British Mycological Society (1967)
123m56, N6

British Mycological Society, 1896
123.56, g, 9M

Botanical Survey of India (1890)
I.44, f2, 9M

National Botanical Research Institute
I.44, f, 9N

Indian Botanical Society
I.44, g, 9N

Report of the Birbal Sahni Institute of Paleobotany (Lucknow)
I : 8.44, d, Br

Life of Linnaeus (1707-1778)
IwL07

Comparative Study of Primary and Secondary roots of Dicotyledons
I8, 1320v3

There seems no class number for Economic botany.

23

J AGRICULTURE

As in mathematics, Ranganathan seems at his best in the schedule of J Agriculture. Enumeration of isolates though not much detailed is quite efficacious. It has been achieved by a simple method of **group notation**—which is nothing short of further splitting an isolate. According to this device Personality, the Agricultural Produce, consists of three digits at least, as follows:

(1) The first digit in the personality isolate is taken from the *utility Array* of plants. It means the use to which the produce is put to i.e., whether it is used as a food, intoxicant, or decoration, and so on.

(2) The second digit is drawn from the *Part Array*. Part array enlists the various (morphological) parts of plants. This digit denotes the part of the plant utilized, viz., whether, fruit, flower, stem, leaf, root, or the whole plant is used for any of the purposes noted in the utility array.

(3) The third digit in the Personality Isolate is got by the *Favoured Category Device*. The most Favoured substance is individualized by adding 1 to the isolate got by combining utility and part array digits. Similarly, digit 2 is added, if it is the second favoured substance.

The formula is:

Utility number + Part number + Favoured category number

Let us illustrate the foregoing abstractions by the example of Rice, whose isolate number in [P] is 381. Rice is a plant whose seed (Part Array) is utilized as human food (utility). It is the most favourite seed food all over the world. Therefore, the (IN) 381 may be analysed as follows:

3 = Food (utility)
8 = Seed (Part)
1 = Most favoured Seed Food

Similarly, for wheat the (IN) is 382 as its use as human seed food, wheat comes next to Rice.

Let us take another example of Tobacco, whose (IN) is 452. Tobacco is a stimulant (utility) whose leaves (part) are used for this purpose next to tea.

4 = Stimulant (utility)
5 = Leaf (Part)
2 = Second favoured leaf stimulant

Since almost all the isolates in the Personality of Agriculture have been enumerated, so the group notation device only explains the rationale behind the enumeration of Personality Isolates. However, when necessary, new isolate numbers may be constructed on these lines. For example, let us make the isolate number for Papyrus. It was a fibrous plant whose stem was used for making writing sheets. Its isolate number may be 7492.

92 is the favoured category digit, as it is the least favoured fibrous stem today.

It may be noted that here favoured category device 91 has already been used in case of Rattan 7491.

[E] means the agricultural problems. Energy occurs in two Rounds. [2E] cum [3P] stands for the secondary agricultural problems and processes.

[2P] is a part or extension of the [E]

Whenever an isolate from [2E] cum [3P] occurs, care should be taken that the isolate from [E] cum [2P] is supplied first, even if it is not explicitly stated. For example, in "Agricultural storage", storage cannot occur unless harvesting is done. Therefore, the formula is:

(Agriculture) : [Harvesting] : [Storage]
J : 7 : 8

It is merely a case of Wall-Picture Principle—there can be no mural without a wall; and no storage without harvesting.

Similarly,

Cold storage of Potatoes
J341 : 7 : 84

Another peculiarity of the schedule lies in the separate enumerations of [E] and [2P] isolates unlike in most other schedules. Here [E] and [2P] isolates have been differentiated from one another. Each isolate in [E] has its own different (or special) [2P]. But as usual there is no need of a comma being put between [E] and [2P] isolates. Further each [2P] has its own set of [2E] isolates. It is another case of **differential facets**.

Soil conservation

Soil is 1 in [E] and conservation is 7 in [2P] of 1[E]. So the class number is:

J : 17

Nitrogenous Manure for pulses

J388 : 241

(Pulse is 388 in [P]. Manure is 2 in [E]; and nitrogenous manure is 41 in the [2P] of 2 Manure in [E].

Collection of Green Manure for Barley

J386 : 21 : 2

Infectious diseases of Apple

J371 : 42

(4 [E] disease has been amplified by [2P] as in L Medicine)

Treatment of virus diseases of Rice

J381 : 423 : 6

If [P_2] i.e., the organ of a plant is also present, its isolate number is the same as the [P_2] of I Botany.

Roots of Potato Plants

J341, 13

Structural diseases of Tissues in Fruit Plants

J37, 12 : 47

Varieties of an agricultural produce may be individualized by (AD):

Basmati Rice

J381B

Parmal Rice

J381P

Stem Diseases of Mexican wheat plants in Punjab

J382M, 14 : 4.4443

Foci in [2P] of 3 and 7 in [E] are the same as in the Part Array of [P]. It is as per instructions given for [2P] isolate at page 2.66. The following examples will make it clear:

Storage of Onion Seeds

J321 : 78 : 8

Here 7 in [E] has been amplified by [2P]8. The digit 8 has been taken from the Part Array of [P] at page 2.64.

Similarly,

Propagation of Rose Stems

J561 : 34

Recovering Groundnut Seeds
J581 : 78 : 2

Transplanting Rose Stems
J561 : 34 : 5

Transplanting Rice Plants
J381 : 397 : 5

Organic Manure for Forests
JB : 25

Dry Forestry for Fruits
JB, 9D, 37

Biological Control of Fungus diseases of Tropical Agriculture Plants of South Asia
J9H : 433 : 6(G).4.9G

Agriculture of Papyrus in the Nile Valley in 500 BC
J7492.6.g1N 'C499

C'Wealth Agricultural Bureaux
J.1N48, f, 9N29

International Institute of Tropical Agriculture (1968)
J9H, 1, d, 9N68

Report of the International Society for Soil Scientist (1924)
J : 1.1, g, 9N24r

Director of the US Department of Agriculture
J.73, w, 9M, 1

Journal of Soil Sciences (UK, 1949+)
J : 1m56, N4

Khad Patrika (1960+)
J : 2m44, N6

Potato Abstracts (UK)
J341am56, N

Punjab Agriculture University (Ludhiana)
J.4443,e4,P

Though it has not been stated explicitly, but [2M] may be added in J : 93 Physiology. Isolates in [2M] are to be got from [P] of E Chemistry—as usual:

Effect of Ammonia in the Physiology of Pulse Plants
J388 : 93 ; 1129

Iron Metabolism in Apple Plants
J371 : 93 ; 182

In these cases [2M] has been taken from the [P] of E Chemistry

Central Potato Research Institute (Shimla: 1935)
J341.44, f, 9N3

24

K ZOOLOGY

Another independent branch of biology which has the animals as object of study.

[P] is the kind of animal—the natural groups. The grouping of animals is on commonly accepted scientific basis. The enumeration of animals is not down to the species level, but only upto the sub-order stage. The further sub-divisions, if required, may be carried out on the same pattern with the help of the *Cambridge Natural History* (Rule K12 p. 1.86). Enumeration of animals upto the stated extent (sub-order stage) is exhaustive. In the Personality Isolates the nomenclature used is technical. To ease the difficulties of the classifier, not adept in Zoology, an alphabetical index of all the Personality Isolates has been given immediately after the schedule (at pages 2.73-2.78). It is also a warning that these natural groups have not been included in the general index.

[P_2] is the body organ. Its isolates are the same as the [P] of L Medicine. But wherever the terms in these two parallel schedules do not match exactly, the analogous terms may be used. For example in case of the wings of birds, there is no term for wings enumerated in the [P] of L. Therefore for "Wings" we can use the term arms. Similarly for feathers, we can use the term hair. But more often than not, this system fails. We do not have terms, (nor even analogous), for tail, crown, trunk, horns in L Medicine!

[E] cum [2P] denote the life process. They are the same as that of G Biology. Two additional energy isolates have been enumerated.

[2M] : It may be remembered that [2M] may be required in case of K : 3 and its sub-divisions.

It is the same as [P] of E Chemistry; others may be obtained by (SD).

Similarly the isolates from K : 12 to K : 18 may require the immediate addition of Space facet.

Books on Paleozoology are classified in H6 Palaeontology.

The general facet formula is:

K[P], [P_2]: [E] [2P]; [2M]

Animal Autopsy
K : 4798

Bird Anatomy
K96 : 2

Vertebrate Taxonomy
K9 : 11

Chemical effect of phosphorus on eyes of birds
K96, 185 : 33E ; 151

Animal Kingdom of Nepal
K : 12.44974

Journal of Indian Fauna, 1912+
K : 12.44mN or K : 12.44m44,N[1]

Oxford Pictorial Encyclopaedia of Animals of South-East Asia (1965)
K : 14.43k56, N

Nervous diseases of mammals
K97, 7 : 4

Rearing among wild animals
K9954 : 591

Courting among primates
K9797 : 595

Effect of Atmospheric temperature on mammal's Physiology
K97 : 30gU284

Bangladesh Journal of Zoology, 1973+
Km44Q71, N7

Journal of Mammalogy (USA, 1919+)
K97m73, N

Indian Journal of Entomology, 1939+
K86m44, N3

Insect Atlas of India (2001)
K86 : 12.44fP1
([T] is upto the (LED))

Indian Association of Systematic Zoologists (Calcutta, 1947)
K : 11.44, g, 9N

Report of the International Committee on Zoological Nomenclature (1895)
K : 11.1 'M95t5

International Council for Bird Preservation (London, 1922)
K96 : 54.1, g, 9N

Anatomical differences between Vertebrates and Invertebrates
K10n9 : 2

Comparative study of Physiology of Aves and Mammals
K960v7 : 3

Collected Physiological Works of Claud Bernard (1813-1878)
K : 3xM13

The Fall of a Sparrow : Autobiography of the
great Indian Orinthologist, Dr. Salim Ali (1896-1987)
K 96 w M 96, 1

Anatomy of Wings of Birds
K96, 163:2

REFERENCE

1. See another example at page p. 1.79, CC-6 (1963).

25

KZ ANIMAL HUSBANDRY

Science of domesticating animals for some economic or esthetic uses.

[P] It is the kind of animal. As in J Agriculture Personality Isolates consist of at least three digits on the similar lines. Isolates in Utility and Part Arrays have been enumerated. Many [P] readymade isolates have also been enumerated; others can be formed by the combination of Utility and Part array schedules.

[P_2] Though not mentioned explicitly, it means the body organ of the animals. It is the same as [P] of L Medicine.

[E] means the problems and techniques of animal husbandry. [2P] is the extension of [E]. Different [E] isolates have their different [2P] and different [2E] isolates. It is yet another case of differential facets. [2E] cum [3P] of KZ : 7 are the same as [2E] cum [3P] of J : 7, i.e., Agricultural Harvesting.

It may be reminded that [2M] may be required in case of KZ : 3. Its isolates are the same as the [P] of E Chemistry. The general facet formula is:

KZ [P], [P_2]: [E] [2P] ; [2M]: [2E] [3P]

Fish Breeding
KZ332 : 6

Horse Feeding
KZ442 :1

Corn Feeding to Horses
KZ442 : 1(J385)

Here [2P] J385 Corn has been got by (SD) as per instructions

Administering Corn Feed to Horses
KZ442 : 1(J385) : 7

Storing of Starch Feed for Dogs
KZ541 : 1(E6892) : 8

In these cases [2E] has been obtained from [2E] of J Agriculture.

Treatment of Fever in Domestic Pigs
KZ334 : 414 : 6

Lungs diseases of traction animals
KZ4, 45 : 4

Administering salt injections to cure infectious diseases in poultry
KZ351 : 42 : 616 ; 4

(Here 4 is [3M] taken from the Personality of [E] Chemistry. See Analogous example at the end of page 1.27 of CC-6).

Immunising dogs against bone cancer
KZ541, 82 : 4725 : 56

Water fasting by camels in deserts
KZ446 : 345.d

Physiology of Nitrogen in Pets
KZ5 : 3 : 150

Cow's Milk
KZ311 : 71

[2P] isolates of KZ : 7 are a peculiar case. They are not only special of 7[E] but also vary according to [P]. To illustrate further:

KZ31 : 7 and KZ35 : 7

have their separate [2P]

Cow's butter milk
KZ311 : 75

Eggs of Hens
KZ351 : 75

Cold Storage of Buffalo Cheese
KZ312 : 78 : 84

Uses of Eggs
KZ351 : 75 : 97

Difference between the Eggs of Hens and Ducks
KZ3510w2 : 75

Diseases of Leg Muscles of Bulls
KZ441, 134-83 : 4

(It seems a doubtful case, as (SID) is seldom employed in other than [P_1] isolates).

British Poultry Science (1960+) : A Journal
KZ35m56, N6

British Goat Society 1879
KZ313.56, g, 9M

Department of Animal Husbandry (Punjab Government)
KZ.4443, w, 9N

International Dairy Federation (Belgium, 1905)
KZ31.1, g, 9N

Directory of Veterinary Surgeons in Punjab started in 1971,
(a hypothetical case)
KZ : 4 : 7n4443, N7

26

L MEDICINE

A study of the human body to prevent and cure human diseases. It is one of the most successful schedules in the CC, yet it is marked for its generality and simplicity.

Systems and Specials occur at the end of the schedule and the (SID) may be frequently required for constructing Personality Isolates.

[P] is the body organ

[E] cum [2P] : Biological problems of human life; working and failure of the human machine.

[2E] cum [3P] : Prevention or treatment or pathology of diseases.

[2M] may be required in case of human physiology : and [3M] in case of substances used as treatment—isolates of both these are to be taken from the [P] of E Chemistry.

Body organs enumerated as subdivisions of 1 are regional divisions (morphological): and isolate numbers 2 to 8 denote functional divisions (anatomical). In case the focus of a term is diffused over both the regional and functional organs, then its isolate number should be got by adding the functional organ number to the regional organ number by (SID) (Rule L 113 page 1.88):

Veins of Leg
L134-36

Head Hair
L18-881

Wrist bone
L166-82

Eye muscles
L185-83

Facial Skin
L181-87

Human Metabolism
L : 33

Sulphur anabolism on human Skin
L87 : 331 ; 161

Effects of Fasting during Pregnancy
L9F : 31 : 94

Functional disorder in eye tissues
L12-185 : 45

Curing structural disorders in skin cells by magnetic therapy
L11-87 : 47 : 627

See rule L111, page 1.88 of CC-6.

Human Pathology
L : 4 : 4

4 [E] Disease is implied when we talk of pathology which occurs in [2E].

(Human) Electrotherapy
L : 4 : 626

Injecting calcium in the Foetus with bone diseases
L9B, 82 : 4 : 616 ; 122

(Here calcium forms [3M] and has been taken from the [P] of E Chemistry)

X-ray diagnosis of bone fracture
L82 : 477 : 3253

Preventing nutrition deficiency in children by diet regulations
L9C : 461 : 642

Blood Analysis by Raman Spectra
L35 : (E : 3, E7)

National Malaria Eradication Programme (NMEP, India)
L : 54261.44 OR L35 : 54261.44

It is a topic of public health. L : 54 is mass prevention of diseases. As per instructions L : 54 has been divided as L : 4. *But it is not clear whether in the class number L : 54261.44* [P] is necessary *as the class number for Malaria, as illustrated, is L35 : 4261.*

State Control on edible oil
L : 523943

(The last three digits come from F Technology, as instructed under L : 523)

State control on pet-dogs
L : 522 541

Law of public health in the U.K.
L : 5 : (Z56)

It may be remembered that whenever a main class digit is amplified by a system or special facet or both, a comma should precede the personality facet. Also a comma should separate the system and special facets, if these happen to occur simultaneously in a subject.

Treating eye diseases in children
L9C, 185 : 4 : 6

Homeopathic treatment of the eye diseases of children
LL, 9C, 185 : 4 : 6

Homeopathic treatment of functional disorders in the eye tissues of children by organotherapy
LL, 9C, 12-185 : 45 : 67

Effect of Iron during pregnancy
L9F : 31 ; 182

[2M] 182 iron has been taken from the [P] of E Chemistry.

Osteopathy system of Medicine
LM7

Acupuncture (2700 BC, China)
LB7

Public hygiene during war times by Ayurvedic Methods
LB, 9V : 55

Important:

There is no example of the (SID) being applied to facets other than first level personality. Therefore, the admissibility of the following two class numbers is doubted:

Tropical Female Lungs Surgery
L9F-9H, 45 : 4 : 7

Homeopathic treatment of eye diseases of old persons during War
LL, 9E-9V, 185 : 4 : 6

Bibliography of Dental Surgery (1999)
L214 : 4 : 7aN9

Bibliography of Female diseases (1995)
L9F : 4aN9

In case of a bibliography [T] should cover the (LED) only.

British Encyclopaedia of public health (1967)
L : 5k56, N6

All India Conference on Pediatrics (1977)
L9C p44, N77

Directory of Dental Surgeons in India (Started in 1975)
L214 : 4 : 7n44, N7

Medica Excerpta
Lam73, N

American Journal of kidney diseases (1981+)
L51 : 4m73, N81

Indian Journal of Homeopathic Medicine (1947)
LLm44, N4

Indian Journal of Public Health (1956)
L : 5m44, N5

Medicine tropical (Spain, 1924+)
L9Hm541, N2

American Journal of Cardiology (1958+)
L32m73, N5

Indian Council of Medical Research
L.44, f, 9N

Report of the Cancer Research Institute (Bombay)
L : 4725.44.B, f, Cr

Maulana Azad Medical College, Delhi
L.4481, e4, M

Duties of the Principal of the Christian Medical College (Ludhiana)
L.4443, e4, C, 1 : 3

Lives of British Great Doctors (Youngest born in 1836)
Lw56, M3

[P_2] of (ACI) should cover the (LED): (See rule 21w5 page 1.47).

A comparative study of Radiotherapy and Thermotherapy
L : 4 : 6240v5

Relation between Prevention and Treatment of human infectious diseases
L : 42 : 50j6

Anatomical Relation between nose and throat
L177 0j41 : 1

Functional Relations between Ear and Throat
L177 0t83 : 3

Folk Medicine
Y : 3 (L)

Index Medicus
2 : 97, (L)

27

LZ PHARMACOGNOSY

It is a science of preparation and study of medicines and drugs. In the CC LZ Pharmacognosy seems an obscure main class, mostly for the reason that it is least illustrated. Not only there are no examples illustrating the use of the schedule, also some of the statements are less than pinpointed. Division into canonical classes is not correct. Then there is no schedule of LZ8 Pharmacy.

At the first instance this main class has been divided into canonical classes:

LZ3	Pharmacology
LZ5	Pharmacopoeia
LZ8	Pharmacy

Facet formula for LZ3 is:

LZ3 [P] : [E] [2P]

It is stated that [P] is to be got by enumeration, whereas actually nothing has been enumerated for [P]. It is presumed that it is the same as the [P] of E Chemistry.

[E] means the action of the drug, and its isolates have been enumerated.

[2P] is the body organ on which drug action takes place. It is to be got by (SD):

Fluoride drugs stimulation of teeth
LZ3 170 : 2(L214)

(170 part of the [P] isolate comes from the [P] of Chemistry).

Benzoids depression of kidneys
LZ371 : 3(L51)

Stomach irritation caused by iron
LZ 3182 : 5(L24)

Depression of Heart by Potassium
LZ3 112 : 3(L32)

Stimulations of heart by calcium chloride
LZ342271 : 2(L32)

Intestinal depression by Magnesium chloride
LZ342171 : 3(L25)

Hydrochloric acid replacements in stomach
LZ33711 : 8(L24)

Antibiotic action of sulphur in blood
LZ161 : 91(L35)

LZ5 Pharmacopoeia means the list of standards for the drugs. The facet formula is

LZ5 [P_1], [P_2]

[P_1] stands for the country and is obviously to be got by (GD)
[P_2] is the kind or order—isolates have been enumerated.

British Pharmacopoeia (BP)
LZ556, 1

Pharmacopoeia Universalle
LZ51, 1

New Nonofficial Remedies (NNR) (USA)
LZ573, 2

British Pharmaceutical Codex
LZ556, 2

Pharmaceutical Journal (UK, 1841)
LZ8m56, M4

American Journal of Pharmacy (1886)
LZ8m56, M8

Eastern Pharmacist (India, 1968+)
LZ8m44, N6

American Society for Pharmacology (1959)
LZ3.73, g, 9N5

American Pharmaceutical Association (1852)
LZ8.73, g, 9M

28

M USEFUL ARTS

This class holds books on applied or industrial arts. For applied aspects of sciences and engineering it is a sort of a hold all miscellaneous class. Impliedly it complements D Engineering. F Technology and even HZ Mining. Making of miscellaneous types of tools, machines and instruments also goes in this main class. Sports and indoor games are also its parts. Its place among the main classes indicates that Ranganathan treats it as the culmination of all the natural sciences. Processes which start with A end in M.

It is one of the most used class but hopelessly inadequate in enumeration. Ranganathan forewarns that "the schedule is only brief and illustrative" (Sec. M01, p. 1.91). The number of such subjects is infinite, he says further (Sec. M02). The schedules of M7 Textile and MJ7 Rope-making are only illustrative. On this analogy, the isolates for other branches of useful arts may be formed. At the first instance the class has been fragmented into canonical divisions. Though it has not been stated but is quite obvious that for subdivisions the main class digit M has been amplified by the **Pseudo subject device**. For example, in:

MD53 Aviation

D53 is air vehicles. Again in MB1 calculating machines, B1 represents the arithmetic. Further in 'MNR Musical Instrument making' NR is the canonical class for Music from the schedule of N Fine Arts. On these analogies other canonical classes can easily be enumerated:

Watch making
MC86

Balance (weighing machine) making
MC11

Geometrical Instruments
MB6

Barometer
MU282

Changes in the schedule should be carefully noted. Starting from 'M3 Domestic Science to M98 Packing' at the end of the first column of page 2.88, a revised schedule has been provided at page 27 of the Annexure. Consequently the energy isolates of MJ7 Rope making are also to be taken from this annexure (p. 27 to CC-6).

Glass Making
M5

Photography
M95

Culinary Art
MA3

Women and Home (1926+)
MA3m56, N2

Spinning silk yarn
M71 : 3 : 1

Weaving jute carpets
M75: 7 : 3

Dyeing Cotton Cloth
M73:1 : 8

Cotton Cloth
M73: 1

Cotton Ginning
M7; 1 : 2

Hemp carding
M7; 6 : 5

Cotton Ropes
MJ71

Twisting Jute Ropes
MJ75 : 2

Wrestling
MY245

The flying Sikh: Life of Milkha Singh
MY225wN40

A Profile of Sachin Tendulkar
MY2141wN74

Life of Mohammad Ali
MY241wN42

A History of Indian Hockey (1910-2000)
MY2143v44 'P00 ← N10

Difference between Athletics and Indoor Games
MY20n3

Indian Textile Bulletin (1955)
M7m44, N55

Indian Journal of Photography (1976+)
M95m44, N7

Sports Review
MYm44, N5

Royal Photographic Society of Great Britain (1853)
M95.56, g, 9M

Olympic Association of India
MY.44, g, 9N

Hockey Association of India
MY2143.44, g, 9N

Playing Chess with Computers
MY322 : (D65, 8(B))

Concept Publishing Company
M16.44, k, C

29

Δ SPIRITUAL EXPERIENCE AND MYSTICISM

From the methodological viewpoint knowledge may be divided as objective and subjective. Objective knowledge is empirical in nature. It is based on direct evidence through sense perception. Anybody with a moderate degree of intellect and required amount of labour may have the access to it. In the Colon Classification the whole of this kind of knowledge has been put in the main classes denoted by the digits a - z, 1 - 9, A - M and N - Z. Subjective knowledge is gained through a sort of inner experience—a direct revelation from the cosmos without sense perception. It transcends logical methods. It is founded on apperception and faith rather than on reason. In library classification this kind of knowledge is usually classed with magic, religion and parapsychology.

In the CC this kind of knowledge has been capsulated in the main class "Δ Spiritual Experience and Mysticism". Ranganathan forewarns that it is self-deluding to call it irrational. Of all the existing schemes, it is only the Colon Classification which has accorded main class status to this kind of knowledge. Perhaps this is one of the reasons that this scheme has been mistaken as strong in Indian subjects. Mysticism and spiritual experiences are not of Indian origin. Being universal they are as much American or European as they are Indian.

Spirituality in India is regarded as highest knowledge—*sarva vidya pratishtha.* The high place given to it is quite evident from its ordinal position fixed by Ranganathan. It is at the cross-roads of sciences and humanities. Ranganathan visualised mystic and spiritual experience as the ultimate source and culmination of all types of subjects: the crown of whole knowledge. Ranganathan envisaged great potentialities in this region of knowledge.

In practical classification it is one of the simple main class. The facet formula is:

Δ [P], [P

[P] is the kind of religion, the domain of spiritual and the mystic experiences. Its isolates are mnemonically parallel to the personality isolates of Q Religion. Isolates in [P] have been enumerated. If some other subject is treated from an occult viewpoint, [P] is to be got by (SD).

[P2] is the agency of such experiences. In the CC it is designated as the entity and its isolates have been enumerated.

[E] cum [2P] : This problem facet involves the methods, techniques and ultimate results of mystic and occult experiences. Isolates have been enumerated.

It is possible for any class of knowledge to be presented from an occult or mystic viewpoint. Only exceptions are N Fine Arts, O Literature and Q Religion. These main classes lie on the border of positivistic and mystic sciences. There is some overlapping, too. Therefore, it is not possible to represent them from mystic viewpoint. Hence class number such as Δ (N), Δ (O) and Δ (Q) are inadmissible as per Rule (page 1.92-1.93), instead, the respective possible class numbers could be:

Nx(Δ)

Ox(Δ)

O, 1x(Δ)

O111, 1x(Δ) or

O : g(Δ)

All class numbers have obvious meanings.

Mystic interpretation of mountains in Zen Buddhism

Δ46, 216 : 7

Voices of disembodied souls according to Hindu mystics

Δ2, 16 : 893

Clairvoyance

Δ: 835

Hallucination

Δ, 16 : 5

Breath control by Hindu mystics

Δ2 : 34

Lakes in mystic experience

Δ, 254

Stars in Hindu astrology

Δ 2, 286 : 864

(Note the double borrowing here for [P_1] 286, first from [P_3] of ND Sculpture and then from [P] of B9 Astronomy).

Similarly

Sun in Astrology
Δ, 283 : 864

An occult study of metals
Δ (E191)

Occult Metabolism
Δ (G : 3)

Mystic manifestation of children diseases
Δ (L9C : 4) : 83

Life of Joan of Arc (1412-31)
Δ 6y7I12

American Federation of Astrologers (1938)
Δ : 864.73, g, 9N

Relation between clairvoyance and astrology
Δ : 835 Ot64

30

N FINE ARTS

N Fine Arts has been divided into canonical classes such as NA Architecture, NB Town Planning, ND Sculpture, NQ Paintings, and NR Music, and many more. It is one of the few main classes where personality spreads itself to a full spectrum. It exists at four levels in many of the canonical classes.

Every canonical class of Fine Arts is first divided by style, then by utility and lastly if, necessary, by part. Style is covered appropriately by (GD) and (CD) forming [P_1] and [P_2] respectively.

[M] is the medium of art and is required only in Paintings, Sculpture and Music. In NR Music, [M] denotes the kind of the musical instrument.

[E] cum [2P] represent the method or the process involved in a particular art. Let us discuss each (CC) separately for particularization:

NA Architecture

The formula is:

NA [P_1], [P_2] [P_3], [P_4] : [E]

Note that there is no comma between [P_2] and [P_3] in accordance with a general rule.[1] [P_1] and [P_2] jointly constitute the style and are denoted by (GD) and (CD) respectively. (CD) is worked upto the century digit only.

Mughal Architecture (16th century India)
NA44, J

Indian Architecture of Victorian Era
NA44, M

European Architecture
NA5
(Here [P_2] is absent)

[P_3] is the kind of building. Its isolates have been enumerated and rest may be got by (SD).

$[P_4]$ is the part of the building:

Hotel Architecture of Victorian India
NA44, M44

Floors of Hotels in Victorian India
NA44, M44, 3

Decoration of urban houses in Renaissance Europe
NA5, J33, 99

Models of elementary schools in 21st century India
NA44, P8(T15) : 8

Models of the walls of elementary schools in 20th century India
NA44, N8(T15), 41 : 8

Architecture of Indian Textile Mills Buildings
NA44, 8(M7)
(Note $[P_2]$ is missing)

Ceiling Architecture
NA, 633

In this case $[P_1]$, $[P_2]$ and $[P_3]$ all are absent. But there may be confusion in retranslation. One may not be sure whether the isolate number 633 is $[P_3]$ or $[P_4]$.

National Library Architecture
NA, 2213

Plans of Mughal Hospital Ceilings
NA44, J8(L), 633 : 3

Location of academic library buildings in Renaissance Europe
NA5, J223 : 1

Journal of Architectural Research (UK, 1970)
NAm56, N7

Academy of Architecture, Bombay
NA.44.B, e4, A

NB Town Planning

In its facet formula and isolates NB Town Planning is closely parallel to NA Architecture.

$[P_3]$ stands for the region of planning whether city, village or town. Isolates have been enumerated.

$[P_4]$ stands for parts of $[P_3]$, i.e., the building to be planned, Isolates have been enumerated.

Theatre Planning in contemporary (21st century) Indian Villages
NB44, P1, 691 : 3

Planning of village markets in Victorian England
NB56, M1, 5 : 3

Location of Public baths in Mughal Towns
NB44, J3, 62 : 1

Town Planning in India today
NB44, P

Provisions of Parks in Metropolitan cities
NB, 7, 66

(Here $[P_1]$ and $[P_2]$ are absent)

Urban and Rural Planning Thoughts (India, 1958+)
NBm44, N5

Guru Ram Das School of Town Planning (Amritsar)
NB.4443.e4, G

Report of the Indian Institute of Town Planners
NB.44, d, 9Nr

Difference between Town and City Planning
NB, 30n5

ND Sculpture

It is the art of casting and moulding three dimensional figures and medals, etc.

$[P_3]$ stands for the object to be cast. Its isolates have been enumerated. Rest can be got by (SD). There is no $[P_4]$ but [M] may be required—the material in which casting is done. The facet formula is:

ND $[P_1]$, $[P_2]$ $[P_3]$; [M] : [E]

Designing human busts in Marble
NB, 18 ; 3 : 4

(Here $[P_1]$ and $[P_2]$ are absent).

Bronze coin casting in Buddhist India
ND44, C71 ; 5 : 5

Buddhistic stone Iconography
ND44, C9(Q) ; 4

Sculpturing Rocks in Wood
ND, 8(H2) ; 1

Pala Sculpture (Bihar)
ND4453, D.

NQ Paintings

$[P_1]$, $[P_2]$ and $[P_3]$ are the same as ND sculpture. Accordingly there is no $[P_4]$. [M] is the medium or the surface on which a painting is drawn.

[E] cum [2P] represent the method or various processes of paintings.

Indian Fresco Water colour Paintings
NQ44 ; 3 : 3

Landscape in Mughal Paintings
NQ44, J3

Preservation of distemper Paintings about animals on Glass
NQ, 5 ; 6 : 6

Comparison of oil and water colours Renaissance Fresco Paintings
NQ5, J ; 3 : 30m4

Life of Picaso
NQ541, NwM81

South Indian Society of Painters (Chennai)
NQ.441, g, S

Bengali National School of Paintings
NQ4475, N

Kangra School of Paintings (18th century)
NQ443682, L

Paintings depicting Hindu myths from the Kangra School of Paintings
NQ443682, L8(Q2 : 8)

Biblical scenes in Gothic Paintings
NQ5, F8(Q6 : 21)

Paintings on Indian History
NQ, 8(V44)

Victorian (British) paintings on Indian History
NQ56, M8(V44)

NR Music

[P_1] and [P_2] constitute the style

[P_2] is the kind of music

[M] is the musical instrument[2]

[E] cum [2P] means the technique of music. Isolates have not been enumerated. They are to be worked out:

Jazz Music
NR73, N

European Orchestra
NR5, 92

Indian Flute
NR44 ; 22

20th century American Kettle-drum dramatic music
NR73, N91 ; 42

Life of Pt. Ravi Shanker
NR44wN20

International Music Centre (1961)
NR.1, d, N6

International Society for contemporary Music (1922)
NR, P.1, g, 9N2

Some topics on art in general:

Art Society of India (1918)
N.44, g, 9N

All India Fine Arts and Craft Society (New Delhi) 1928
N.44, g, 9N2

Bombay Art Society
N.44.B, g, B

Functions of Lalit Kala Akademi (1954)
N.44, d, 9N5 : 2

International Association of Art (1949)
N.1, g, 9N49

Rajeshvari Kala Sangam (Jalandhar)
N.4443, e4, R

Art Journal (USA, 1941+)
Nm73, N4

History of Indian Cinema (1999)
NW44v'N9

National School of Drama (New Delhi)
NT.44, e4, 9N

Kathak Dance
NS44, J

In case of collection of Art works the digit x should be added to the ultimate class numbers. It should further be amplified by (AD) using the name of the artist. To it a work facet preferably got again by (AD), may be added in case of a particular artifacet.

Leonardo da Vinci's Monalisa
NQ52, JxL, M

Last Supper by Leonardo da Vinci
NQ52, JxL, L

Collection of Rabindranath Tagore's Paintings
NQ4475, NxT

Beethoven's *Namensfeir* (an orchestral Music)
NR55, M92xB, N

REFERENCES

1. See Satija M.P., *Epistle to Dean Shera on the Brevity of Notation in Colon Classification*, Amritsar, Rajat, 1979, p. 31.
2. It may look very odd that the musical instruments have been enumerated under the matter facet. But it is quite appropriate according to the theory of music that music already is there in the cosmos. It is only through the medium of instruments that it is made audible.

31

O LITERATURE

It is one of the peculiar but simple main classes. Here only personality category exists : all other categories are absent. Personality occurs at four levels—helping to individualize specifically every literary work. Therefore, this schedule works with ease and simplicity in assigning co-extensive class numbers to the works of creative literature. On the other hand it seems hopelessly inadequate in case of critical literature. Literary forms enumerated are primitively broad. Species or genre of literature have not been enumerated, nor they can be improvised by (SD). Ranganathan tenders his own arguments in self-defence—meaning that the omissions have been knowingly made (Rule 02, pp. 1.98-1.99). Notwithstanding Ranganathan's own defence, the CC has incurred a big disadvantage by not dividing the Form facet further into species.

The CC arranges literature first by language, followed consecutively by the divisions of form, author and work. Each division is designated by a level of personality in the above order. Thus the facet formula is:

$$O[P_1], [P_2] [P_3], [P_4]$$

$[P_1]$ stands for the **language** of the literature. Its isolates are to be taken from the common schedule of languages given at page 2.26.

$[P_2]$ stands for the **form** of literature viz., Drama, Poetry or Fiction. Isolates have been enumerated in the schedule at page 2.94.

$[P_3]$ stands for the **author** facet to be got by (CD). In case of an individual author (CD) is to be got by the exact year of birth of the author. In case of anthologies (CD) is worked to the (LED) covered by the year of birth of the youngest author.

$[P_4]$ stands for the individual, named **work** of a given author. It may be got by Group Notation or by (AD).

Method of applying group notation deserves an explanation:

(1) If the number of works of an author is upto eight, then these may be arranged in the sequence they are published, viz., 1, 2, 3 upto 8.

(2) In case the number of works of an author is upto 64, then these works are arranged in eight groups as follows:

Group No.	*Item No.*							
	1	*2*	*3*	*4*	*5*	*6*	*7*	*8*
1	1	2	3	4	5	6	7	8
2	9	10	11	12	13	14	15	16
3	17	18	19	20	21	22	23	24
4	25	26	27	28	29	30	31	32
5	33	34	35	36	37	38	39	40
6	41	42	43	44	45	46	47	48
7	49	50	51	52	53	54	55	56
8	57	58	59	60	61	62	63	64

From the above table each work is denoted by at least **two digits.** First digit stands for the group and the second for the item number in that group. Thus the first work is denoted as 11 meaning the first work of the first group. The 25th work is given the work number 41, meaning the first work of the fourth group. Similarly, the 17th work is denoted as 31: the 31st as 47 : and 64th work as 88.

(3) If the number of works of an author is more than 64 upto 512, then all the works are divided into eight groups of 64 works each. Each work is denoted by the **three digits**. The first digit stands for the **group number**, the second for the **sub-group** and the third digit for the **item number** in the sub-groups:

Group No. 1

Sub-group	*Item No.*							
	1	*2*	*3*	*4*	*5*	*6*	*7*	*8*
1	1	2	3	4	5	6	7	8
2	9	10	11	12	13	14	15	16
3	17	18	19	20	21	22	23	24
4	25	26	27	28	29	30	31	32
5	33	34	35	36	37	38	39	40
6	41	42	43	44	45	46	47	48
7	49	50	51	52	53	54	55	56
8	57	58	59	60	61	62	63	64

Group No. 2

Sub-group	*Item No.*							
	1	*2*	*3*	*4*	*5*	*6*	*7*	*8*
1	65	66	67	68	69	70	71	72
2	73	74	75	76	77	78	79	80
3	81	82	83	84	85	86	87	88
4	89	90	91	92	93	94	95	96
5	97	98	99	100	101	102	103	104
6	105	106	107	108	109	110	111	112
7	113	114	115	116	117	118	119	120
8	121	122	123	124	125	126	127	128

Group No. 3

Sub-group	*Item No.*							
	1	*2*	*3*	*4*	*5*	*6*	*7*	*8*
1	129	130	131	132	133	134	135	136
2	137	138	139	140	141	142	143	144
3	145	146	147	148	149	150	151	152
4	153	154	155	156	157	158	159	160
5	161	162	163	164	165	166	167	168
6	169	170	171	172	173	174	175	176
7	177	178	179	180	181	182	183	184
8	185	186	187	188	189	190	191	192

Group No. 4

Sub-group	*Item No.*							
	1	*2*	*3*	*4*	*5*	*6*	*7*	*8*
1	193	194	195	196	197	198	199	200
2	201	202	203	204	205	206	207	208
3	209	210	211	212	213	214	215	216
4	217	218	219	220	221	222	223	224
5	225	226	227	228	229	230	231	232
6	233	234	235	236	237	238	239	240
7	241	242	243	244	245	246	247	248
8	249	250	251	252	253	254	255	256

Group No. 5

Sub-group	*Item No.*							
	1	*2*	*3*	*4*	*5*	*6*	*7*	*8*
1	257	258	259	260	261	262	263	264
2	265	266	267	268	269	270	271	272
3	273	274	275	276	277	278	279	280
4	281	282	283	284	285	286	287	288
5	289	290	291	292	293	294	295	296
6	297	298	299	300	301	302	303	304
7	305	306	307	308	309	310	311	312
8	313	314	315	316	317	318	319	320

Group No. 6

Sub-group	Item No.							
	1	*2*	*3*	*4*	*5*	*6*	*7*	*8*
1	321	322	323	324	325	326	327	328
2	329	330	331	332	333	334	335	336
3	337	338	339	340	341	342	343	344
4	345	346	347	348	349	350	351	352
5	353	354	355	356	357	358	359	360
6	361	362	363	364	365	366	367	368
7	369	370	371	372	373	374	375	376
8	377	378	379	380	381	382	383	384

Group No. 7

Sub-group	Item No.							
	1	*2*	*3*	*4*	*5*	*6*	*7*	*8*
1	385	386	387	388	389	390	391	392
2	393	394	395	396	397	398	399	400
3	401	402	403	404	405	406	407	408
4	409	410	411	412	413	414	415	416
5	417	418	419	420	421	422	423	424
6	425	426	427	428	429	430	431	432
7	433	434	435	436	437	438	439	440
8	441	442	443	444	445	446	447	448

Group No. 8

Sub-group	Item No.							
	1	*2*	*3*	*4*	*5*	*6*	*7*	*8*
1	449	450	451	452	453	454	455	456
2	457	458	459	460	461	462	463	464
3	465	466	467	468	469	470	471	472
4	473	474	475	476	477	478	479	480
5	481	482	483	484	485	486	487	488
6	489	490	491	492	493	494	495	496
7	497	498	499	500	501	502	503	504
8	505	506	507	508	509	510	511	512

In this case the first work is denoted as 111 meaning the first item in the first sub-group of the first group. Similarly the second work is denoted as 112; and the 512th work as 888. The 419th work will be denoted by 753 meaning that it is the 3rd item in the 5th sub-group of the 7th group. Similarly 100th work of an author will be denoted by 254 meaning and group, 5th subgroup and 4th item in 5th subgroup.

Despite this much of calculations, sometimes it is very difficult to ascertain the serial number of a work. Not to speak of the classifier or the general public, even the authors sometimes fail to assign a strict chronological order to their works. It is not unusual that the works be published in some other order of their writing : Sometimes a work is never published in an author's life time. A work may also be published in different editions and versions. Hence it is very difficult to determine the strict chronological order of a work. "IN PRACTICE", feels Ranganathan, "THIS METHOD OF NUMBERING INVOLVES MUCH WORK. IT IS FELT THAT THE BENEFIT DERIVED BY THE READERS FROM SUCH AN ARRANGEMENT IS NOT ADEQUATE ENOUGH TO JUSTIFY ALL THE TROUBLES AND TIME INVOLVED. THEREFORE, AN ALTERNATIVE METHOD AVAILABLE IS TO CONSTRUCT THE ISOLATE NUMBERS OF A WORK BY ALPHABETICAL DEVICE" (emphasis added)

Shakespeare's Hamlet
O111, 2J64, H

Tess of the d' Ubervilles by Thomas Hardy (Birth 1862)
O111, 3M62, T

Chitta Lahu a novel by Nanak Singh
O153, 3M97, C

Milton's Paradise Lost
O111, 1K08, P

In case of a critical work or an evaluation of an author, the ultimate number should be sharpened by adding ":g" :

Guy de Maupassant—an evaluation
O122, 3M50 : g

A critical evaluation of Shakespeare's Hamlet
O111, 2J64, H : g

Prem Chand's Gaudan : An Appraisal
O152, 3M80, G : g

"g" may further be sharpened by (SD) if the evaluation is from some particular viewpoint:

Psychology of Hamlet
O111, 2J64, H : g(S)

Robert Browning's Men and Women, as Love Poetry
O111, 1M12, M : g(S : 55)

A Psychological of Shakespeare's Women Character
O111, 2J64 : g(S55)

Hindu superstitions in the poetry of *Mahakavi* Tulsi Das (birth 1534)
O152, 1J34x : g(Y73(Q2) : 354)

John Donne as a Metaphysical Poet
O111, 1J72 : g(R3)

In the above two examples it may be noted that no work facet is involved, hence [P_4] is absent. Similarly,

John Keats as a poet of Aesthetics
O111, 1L92 : g(R5)

Pope's Rape of the Lock, as a Mirror of contemporary Society
O111, 1K88, R : g(Y)

Collected poems of Thomas Hardy
O111, 1M62x

Collected works of Thomas Hardy
(He was both a novelist and a poet)
O111xM62

(Position of (ACI) digit x may be noted in the above two cases)

In case of anthologies, or collected biographies, the (CD) is to be worked upto the (LED) covered by the year of birth of the youngest author:

Anthology of Punjabi poems, Youngest author born in 1947
O153, 1xN5

Lyrical Ballads by William Wordsworth (1770-1850)
and T.S. Coleridge (1772-1834)
O111, 1xL7

Biography of Shakespeare
O111, 2J64w

Autobiography of Jai Shanker Prasad
O152, 1M90w, 1

Collected biographies of Wordsworth (1770-1850), Coleridge (1772-1834).
Walter Scott (1771-1832) and Byron (1788-1824)
O111, 1wL9

Byron is the youngest. But if the collection or biographies are from some subject viewpoint then w or x may be sharpened by (SD) and then by (CD). (Rule O9wn page 1.103)

Collection of religious poems in Hindi
(Youngest author born in 1893)
O152, 1x(Q)M9

Collection of Punjabi love poems
(Youngest author born in 1942)
O153, 1x(S : 55)N5

Mystical writings of DH Lawrence
O111, 3M75x(Δ)

Biographies of the love poets of the world
(Youngest born in 1933)
O, 1w(S : 55)N3

Treatment of Child Psychology in the works of Dostovesky (b. 1821)
O142, 3M21 : g(S1)

Oxford dictionary of English quotations
O111xk

Dictionary of Political sayings
O111x(W)k

Dictionary of moral maxims from Sanskrit Poetry
O15, 1x(R4)k

A title index of Shakespeare's poems
O111, 1J64d

An index of the first lines of poems by Alfred Tennyson
O111, 1M09e

(These additional (ACI)s d and e have been added according to Rule 09 page 1.102)

History of English Literature upto 1995
O111v 'N9

British Journal of 19th century English literature
O111, Mn56, N

Indian Journal of English Literature (1931)
O111m44, N7

Sahitya Akademi
O.44, g, 9N

Amritsar Literary Society
O.4443.A, g, A

Walt Whitman Review (USA), 1954+)
O111A, 1M12m73, N5

(For American English O111 has been sharpened by AD).

Cambridge Bibliography of English Literature upto 1920
O111aN3

Hamlet : a critical anthology (youngest critic born in 1949)
O111, 2J64, H : gx N5

An evaluation of Benedetto Croce (1866-1952)'s criticism on Shakespeare
O111, 2J64 : gxM66

A bibliography (published in 2000) on Research in Shakespeare
O111, 2J64 : faP1

Hamlet Studies : A journal of Research on
the Tragedy of Hamlet, (1978—)
O111, 2J64, Hm1, N7

32

P LINGUISTICS

Previously known as Philology, linguistics is the science of language. The schedule of P linguistics is difficult and easy both. The main difficulty arises in [P_2], which consists of not one but two facets—a unique case. These are variant facet and the stage facet. Variant of a language means the geographical variations in a given language—the different dialects of a language at a given time. It is denoted by 9D which is further sharpened by (GD), i.e., the area in which a particular dialect is spoken.

[P_2] also covers the stages of a language—which means the change caused in a given language by time. Every language changes with time. Such changes are very slow and are perceptible with time. Such changes are very slow and are perceptible only after centuries. It is only denoted by the century of epoch. Obviously stage is denoted by (CD). AND IF BOTH THE STAGE AND THE VARIANT FACETS ARE PRESENT SIMULTANEOUSLY THEN THE [P] SHOULD BE FOLLOWED FIRST BY STAGE AND THEN BY VARIANT. A COMMA SHOULD BE INTERPOSED BETWEEN THE STAGE AND VARIANT FACETS. (Rule P92Z page 1.105).

[P] is the language under study

[P_3] is the linguistic element.

[E] cum [2P] are the linguistic problems.

The formula is:

P [Language], [Stage], [Variant], [Element] : [Problem]

$$\frac{\text{P Language}}{[P_1]}, \quad \frac{\text{(CD), 9D [Area]}}{[P_2]}, \quad \frac{\text{Element}}{[P_3]}$$

English Language
P111

Modern English
P111, J

(Here in [P_2] variant is absent, only stage is present)

Dialects of English
P111, 9D

Nottinghamshire Dialect of English
P111, 9D56176

Nottinghamshire Dialect of Modern English
P111, J, 9D56176

Clause analysis of London Dialect of Modern English
P111, J, 9D56124, 5:33

In case of Jargon the above formula is bit reversed : 9J is amplified by (GD) and to it is added (CD) digit. (GD) and (CD) are separated by a comma.

Anglo-Indian Jargon
P111, 9J44, L

Contemporary Lakhnavi Urdu
(Lucknow Dialect of contemporary Urdu)
P168, N, 9D445292

A dictionary of contemporary Canadian-French phrases
P122, N, 9D72, 4 : 4k

Sri Lankan dialect of Tamil
P31, 9D4498

Dialects of Korean Language
P495, 9D

[Korean Language has been got by (GD)]

A Linguistic study of the Wu Language
(Chinese dialect spoken in Chekiang)
P41, 9D4113

Semasiology of Thai Dialects
P433, 9D : 4

Rules for constructing isolate numbers for **artificial and other languages** not enumerated in the schedule at pages 2.26-2.27, have been discussed in the chapter 5 of language isolates at page 1.54.

Grammar of Bihari Language
P1594473 : 5

A study of verbs of Korean Language
P495, 35

Old Hindi Phonology
P152, D : 1

Middle Hindi words
P152, F3

It may be noted that if $[P_3]$ immediately follows the stage facet then there is no need of comma between $[P_2]$ and $[P_3]$.

Analysis of simple clauses in Vedic Sanskrit
P15, A561 : 33

Borrowed words in Modern Hindi
P152, M305

Vowel pronunciation in old French
P122, A11 : 1

Chhatisgarhi Hindi Phrases
P152, 9D447111, 4

There is a peculiar exception to the facet formula in the co-occurrence of energy isolates from 4 to 58 and the element number, i.e. $[P_3]$ 3. In such cases the **element number, i.e., 3 in $[P_3]$ is to be omitted**.

English Dictionary
(A dictionary gives meanings of words)
P111, 3 : 4k
= P111 : 4k

Borrowing of words in Punjabi Language
P153, 3 : 58 = P153 : 58

Coining new words in Russian Language
P142 : 53

A dictionary of Phrase meanings of English Jargon
P111, 9J, 4 : 4k

Hindi *Kahavte* (Proverbs)
P152, 6 : 4

Bilingual dictionaries pose no problem in the CC. In the class number only the first language, i.e., the languages in which the words are given is considered as personality. The language in which the meanings are given is considered the language of exposition which is represented in the **Book Number**.

Sanskrit-Hindi Dictionary
P15 : 4k

Sanskrit-English Dictionary
P15 : 4k

Old German-English Dictionary
P113, D : 4k

Specialised subject dictionaries are to be put in their respective subjects.

Dictionary of Science in English
A : (P111)k

English-Punjabi dictionary of Political Science Terms
W : (P111)k

":(G)" is to be put for comparative study of languages (Rule P9 : (G), page 1.106).

Comparative study of Dravidian Languages
P3 : (G)

Some of the isolates in [P_3] namely 11 and 15 have their own Common Isolates:

Nasal Mixed Vowels of the English Language
P111, 11508

Here "08" is the Common Isolate standing for Nasal. Being a (CI) it has been directly added to the ultimate class number P111, 115 Mixed vowels of the English language. It means that 08 is a special kind of common isolate.

Lateral bilabial consonants of Pakistani Punjabi
P153, 9D44Q7, 15802

Predental Voiced consonants
P, 166

Fricative predental voiced consonants
P, 16604

Plosive closed unvoiced consonants
P, 17101

Circular rolled unvoiced consonants of Burmese Language
P438, 17203

Grammatical aspects of composing English poetry
P111, 71 : 2

Figure of speech in novels-a linguistic study
P, 73 : 75

Another very peculiar rule exists in the grammatical study of Vedas—in Vedic Sanskrit P15, A. In this case the digit A is to be preceded by at least two digits, the first digit standing for the particular Veda and the second for its version. These digits are to be taken from the chapter Q Religion in part 3, page 3.22.

Grammar of Sama Veda
P15, 31A : 2

The digits 31 preceding A have been taken from Q131 Sama Veda.

Tense in Vajasaneya
P15, 26A : 27

Taittiriya word composition
P15, 25A3 : 291
3 is [P_3] here
Vedic Sanskrit Adverbs
P15, A36

Teaching of any language like teaching of any other subject will go to T Education.

Teaching of English language to foreigners in England
T35 : 3(P111).561
Teaching of Hindi in Secondary Schools
T2 : 3(P152)
Teaching of mother-tongue in elementary schools
T15 : 3(P1)
Teaching of classical languages in universities through mother-tongue
T4 : 3(P8), 31
A comparative study of phrases and clauses
P, 40m5
Difference in the translation technique of simple and complex sentences of English language
P111, 6010w7 : 795
Journal of Language of Poems (USA, 1972+)
P, 71m73, N7
Anuvad (1964+)
P : 795m44, N64
All India Seminar on Linguistics (New Delhi, 1975)
Pp44, N75
Bibliography on Linguistic Research in India (1973)
P:f.44aN7
A Comparative Study of Indian Languages
P44 : (G)
A Comparative Grammar
P : 5 : (G)

FURTHER READING

Ranganathan, S.R., "Classification of Linguistics"; reported by M.A. Gopinath, *Lib. Sc. with a Slant to Documentation*, 1(3), Sept. 1964 : 197-223.

33

Q RELIGION

It is one of the simple schedules in the CC. In some cases of religions of Indian origin, especially Hindu religion, the provision exists relatively for minute classification. The facet formula is:

Q[P] : [E] [2P]

[P] is the religion itself. Its isolates have been enumerated mostly. Others may be got by (GD) or (CD)—such places have been indicated in the schedule.

[E] cum [2P] enlists the religious practices and beliefs

Rigvedic Mythology
Q11 : 1

Religious practices of Ahmadiya Muslims
Q78M9 : 4

Kathaka Grahyasutra
Q122 : 42

Kanva Dharmasutra
Q128 : 44

Saunakiya Samhita
Q141 : 21

Taittirya Gotrapravara
Q125 : 46

Religious rites in Parsis's marriage
Q8451 : 427

Bible
Q6 : 21

Q:2 is scriptures and it has to be further subdivided according to the religion. In part 3 of the CC, Ranganathan has enumerated in detail the religious classics mostly Indian, and a few foreign. Their class numbers have been obtained with the help of the Classic Device. On page 3.32 the number for the Bible and its various books have been enumerated as follows:

Q6 : 21	Bible
Q6 : 22	Old Testament
Q6 : 2225	Songs of Solomon
Q6 : 23	New Testament
Q6 : 231	St. Matthew
Q6 : 235	Acts
Q6 : 294	Apocrypha

Similarly,

Sri Guru Granth Sahib (Sikh Scriptures)
Q8441 : 2

Sri Guru Nanak Dev Ji—The Founder of Sikh Religion
Q8441 : 33

Biography of Jesus Christ
Q6 : 33y7

Lives of Biblical saints
Q6 : 332y7

The Holy Quran
Q7 : 2

Traditions in Zen Buddhism
Q4596 : 26

Sun Worship in Ancient India
Q1 : 414(B9)

In case of Q : 38 Sthala Purana, [E] 38 is to be further amplified by (GD). It is to be divided as the Geographical isolate 44.

Sthala Puranas of South Indian (Space Isolate for South India is 441)
Q2 : 381

Sthala Puranas of Kanshi
Q2 : 385213

Sthala Purana of Madura
Q2 : 38134

(The (SI) for Madura is 44134 and for Kanshi it is 445213)

Hindu Temples
Q2 : 45

Influence of scriptures on Mythology
Q : 10r2

A comparative study of the sacred books of Buddhists and Jains
Q3 0m4 : 2

Difference between Roman Catholic and Protestants Traditions
Q620w3 : 26

Catholic Digest (India, 1960+)
Q62m44, N6

Hindu Vishva (India, 1966+)
Q22m44, N6

Journal of Religion (US, 1882)
Qm73, M8

Journal of Sikh Studies (India, 1974+)
Q8441m44, N74

Tradition: Journal of Orthodox Jewish Thought (USA, 1958+)
Q5m73, N5

International Theosophical Society (1877)
QM : 68.1, g, 9M

YMCA (India)
Q6 : 6811.44, g, 9N

World Council of Churches (1948+)
Q6:6.d.1, g, 9N4

34

R PHILOSOPHY

Now-a-days philosophy is more an applied subject—a sort of tool or methodology. In the CC it has been divided first on the canonical basis, such as Logic, Epistemology, Metaphysics and Ethics. Various systems of philosophy have been put in R6 to R8. R6 has been reserved for the most favoured system. Inevitably in the CC it is meant for the Indian Philosophy. R7 is meant for the second favoured system. Philosophies of all other nations have been placed in R8, which is sharpened by (GD). **It is a typical case where the systems have been got by (GD) instead of (CD)**. There is no way to assign a succinct class number to various philosophical concepts such as Existentialism, Pragmatism, except to put them in the philosophy of the country where enunciated first:

Symbolic Logic
R14

Fundamental categories of knowledge
R299

Various postulates about categories may be got by (CD)—treating them as systems:

Aristotle's views on categories
R299C

Ranganathan's Five Fundamental Categories
R299N5

Philosophies of various subjects are put in the subjects themselves, where R is applied as an Energy Facet got by (SD):

Philosophy of History
V : (R)

Philosophy of Mathematics
B : (R)

But the Philosophical aspects of the theory of Religion are put in R3

Metaphysics, and further fitted with a [P_2] got by (SD). Thus the facet formula for R3 Metaphysics is:

R3 [P], [P_2]

[P] is regarded as view. Its isolates have been enumerated.

[P_2] is the subject matter of metaphysics and is obviously got by (SD):

Christian Philosophy
R3, (Q6)

Christian Humanism Philosophy
R39(Y), (Q6)

Metaphysics of number theory
R3, (B12)

Economic Value
R37, (X)

Similarly the facet formula for Ethics is

R4 [P], [P_2]

[P] may be taken as the sphere or jurisdiction of Ethics

[P_2] is named as the controlling view, or the limiting factor.

Family Ethics of Royalty
R42, (Y51)

State Ethics in a representative democracy
R43W61

Ethics in Indoor Games
R463

Ethics about temperance among the leaders
R413, (Y48)

Buddhist kindness towards Animals
R47, (Q4)

Conduct of Brahmins towards Animals
R47, (Y5923)

Ethics of Librarianship
R442

Ethics of Economists
R44X

The facet formula for R6 **Indian Philosophy** is:

R6 [P_1], [P_2]

[P_1] covers various schools of Indian Philosophy

[P_2] (1) lists the sources of Indian Philosophy, applicable only from R65 to R6893:

(2) other views in Indian philosophy, are to be taken from R itself

Yoga Philosophy
R635

Mahayana Philosophy
R6945

Bhagvad Gita
R68, 6

Mahabharata
R68, 8

Bhagvata
R6893, 7

Brahma Sutra
R65, 5

Theory of Epistemology according to Hindu Philosophy
R61, 2

Symbolic Logic of Purva Mimansa
R64, 14

Vaisesika Inductive Logic
R621, 11

Probability in Yoga Philosophy
R635, 198

Metaphysics in Bhatta Mimansa
R641, 3

Vedanta Logic
R65, 91

Here $[P_2]$9 has been divided as R, (R1 is Logic)

Vaisnava Epistemology
R672, 92

Theory of Aesthetics according to Jaina School of Philosophy
R693, 95

R8 is to be sharpened by (GD) to get the philosophical system of various countries.

British Philosophy
R856

American Philosophy
R873

Greek Philosophy
R851

Greek Epistemology
R851, 2

And those who do not place Indian Philosophy in R6, may put it as:
R844

Difference between inductive and Deductive Logic
R110w2

Life of British Philosopher John Lock (1632-1704)
R856wK32

Collected philosophical works of Australian Philosopher
Samuel Alexander (1859-1938)
R88xM59

Journal of Philosophical Logic (Netherlands, 1972+)
R1m44, N7

Indian Institute of Philosophy (1916)
R.44, d, 9N1

Association of Symbolic Logic (USA, 1936)
R14.73, g, 9N3

35

S PSYCHOLOGY

S Psychology is a relatively simple schedule. There are no exceptional rules. Systems also occur and have been enumerated in the end. [2E] cum [3P] facet also occurs. The Facet formula is:

S (System Facet), [P] : [E] [2P] : [2E] [3P]

[P] is the individual human being. Connotations of obvious terms such as child, adolescent, etc., have been explained, though these may rarely be needed. (SID) may be required frequently.

[E] cum [2P] enlist psychological activities and processes.

[2E] cum [3P] isolates mostly pertains to phychophysics and physiological psychology. These are only for 2 and 3 in [E]. It means it is a **differential facet**.

Cognition in a new born baby
S11 : 4

Psychology of Genius Girls
S25-61

Psychology of Librarians
S4 (2)

S4 is to be divided by (SD)

Psychology of Lady Doctors
S4(L)-55

Personality of Philosophers
S4(R) : 7

Personality of Logicians
S4(R1) : 7

A study of Fear among the Europeans
S75 : 526

Here S7 has been subdivided by (GD)

Endurance in Rural people—a Psychological Study
S831 : 793

Here S8 has been sub-divided as Y Sociology.

Gypsies brain—a psycho study
S8738 : 12

Child Cerebrum—a psychological study
S1 : 1221

Physiological Psychology of color sense among toddlers
S12 : 255 : 3

Hindu Social Psychology
S873(Q2)

Psycho analytical study of Mongolian People
SM9, 873(P41)

History of various Psychological Schools of Thoughts (brought up to 1975)
SAv 'N7

Experimental psychology of the Brain of abnormal boys
SM, 21-6 : 12

Field psychology of left handed females
SN8, 55-6916

Psychometry
S : 3 : 6

Statistical Psychology
S : (B28)

Educational Psychology
SobT

International Psycho-analytical Association (1908)
SM9. 1, g, 9N

Indian Psychological Abstracts (1972+)
Sam44, N

Journal of Experimental Social Psychology (USA, 1963+)
SM, 8m73, N6

Indian Journal of Experimental Psychology (1976)
SMm44, N6

36

T EDUCATION

Though quite mechanical in operation, it is one of the interesting schedules. Depth classification is possible without any difficulty. There are no exceptions except the occurrence of rare [$2P_2$] facet. Systems also occur. The formula is:

T [P] : [E] [2P], [2P2]

[P] is constituted of various types of educands—the level or kind of students.

[E] is constituted of educational techniques or problems. [2P] covers the subject taught—obviously to be got by (SD). A few isolates have also been enumerated.

[$2P_2$] enlists methods or physical medium of teaching.

T (system), [Educand] : [Problem] [Subject], [Technique]

Teaching of Algebra in Secondary Schools
T2 : 3(B2)

Teaching of Algebra in Secondary Schools by Audiovisual method
T2 : 3 (B2), 1

Curriculum in Punjabi Literature for honours students
T43 : 2(O153)

Home Science Curriculum for female college students
T42-55 : 2(MA)

Ability test for Scientific researchers by viva voce
T48 : 5(A), 7

Home work in Colon Classification to Post Graduate Students
T45 : 4(2 : 51N3), 1

Headmaster of Kindergarten elementary school
TL8, 15 : 87

(Here as per instructions 8[E] has been sub-divided as X : 8)

Headmistress of the Holy Heart Kindergarten Elementary School, Amritsar
TL8, 15.4443.A, d, H, 1

Executive Council of a University
T4 : 82

Financial administration in Indian Universities
T4 : 8D.44

Wardha Secondary School Hostels
TN3, 2 : 72

Merrill-Palmer Intelligence Test
T : 5, IN31

Teaching Hindu Religion to the Hindu Students
T9(Q2) : 3(Q2)

Difference between the curriculum of male and female students
T510w5 : 2

Influence of curriculum on teaching techniques
T : 30r2

Teaching of Linguistics
T : 3(P)

Indian Association of Teachers of Library and Information Science
T : 3(2). 44, b, g, 9N

Teaching of mother-tongue by visual methods to illiterates
T38 : 3(P1), 15

Examining vocational students in foreign languages
T9 (Y4) : 5(P5), 5

Forum of Education, (Australia, 1941+)
Tm8, N4

Times Educational Supplement (U.K., 1910+)
Tm56, N1

Report of the Education Commission (1957)
T.44 'N57t

Research in Education in India
T : f.44

National Council of Educational Research and Training (NCERT) (1961)
T.44, f, 9N6

Montessori International Association (1925)
TN1. 1, g, 9N2

Association of Commonwealth Universities
T4. 1N48, g, 9N4

Commonwealth Universities Handbook
T4. 1N48n56, N

International Association of University Professors and
Lecturers (France, 1944)
T4, b.1, g, 9N4

National Institute of Basic Education (New Delhi, 1956+)
TN3.44, d, 9N5

All India Seminar on Teaching of Indian History (1970)
T : 3(V44)p44, N70

Conference of Punjab College Teachers (1995)
T42, bp4443, N95

Report of the University Education Commission (1948-1949: Chairman, S. Radhakrishnan)
T4.44 'N48t5

37

U GEOGRAPHY

Geography is an ever expanding subject which encompasses under its umbrella many seemingly varied topics. Its boundaries cross and criss-cross with economics, sociology, civilization and culture, travels, commerce, geography, geology, and many more. Its vast expanse involves interaction between nature and society for rational use of natural resources. Ranganathan truly says that it is an elusive subject, which is ancient and modern, both. It is a bridge between the human society and the world of nature. Therefore, it is very difficult to define its scope, except by enumeration.

The first division of U Geography is on canonical lines. But strangely enough such a rich and varied subject has been sparsely enumerated. Only [P] has been given. There is no [E] even, not to speak of [M] and other levels of [P]. Of course [S] and [T] may be used often, which are to be taken from their respective schedules. Ranganathan advises that in case of U6 Economic Geography and U8 Travels [T] should be the (LED) covered:

Rainfall in India in the summer of 1982
U2855.44 'N82 'n3

Rainfall in Indian mountains in the winter of 1981
U2855.44.g7 'N81 'n7

Physical Geography of the Himalayas
U2.4.g7H

Wind velocity in Gangetic valley in the nights of 1981
U2831.44.g1G 'N81'd

Human Geography of the Bengal Forests
U47.4462.f

Railway Routes in the Nile Valley
U6415.6.g1N

Voyages in the Indian Ocean brought upto 1995
U8.95 'N9

Maps of Indian Industrial Resources (1947)
U672.44fN5

A Textbook of Economic Geography of India
U6.44

Human Migration in Snow Times
U42 'p8

Air Routes in India in 2000
U6435.44 'P00

Air Routes in India brought upto 1999
U6435.44 'N9

Political map of India brought upto 1970s
U5.44.fN7

How Nature makes seasons
U16

Mathematical equation of atmospheric pressure and temperature
U2820t4 : (B)

Weather forecasting for Agriculture
U2891 obJ

Geopolitics of Punjab
WOgU.4443

Life of William Dampier (1651-1715)
U8wK51

Journal of the Geographical Society of India
Um44, N3

Geographical Magazine (UK, 1935+)
Um56, N3

Royal Geographical Society (1843)
U.56, g, 9M

President of the Geographical Society of India (1933)
U.44, g, 9N3, 1

Indian Association of Mathematical Geography (1970)
U1.44, g, 9N

National Atlas Organization, Calcutta (1956)
U11.44, d, 9N5

Punjab Tourism Corporation
U8.4443, k, 9N

World Meteorological Organisation (1873)
U28.1, g, 9M

Fodor's Guide to India
U8.44n56, N

38

V HISTORY

In the CC, V History is rather an interesting main class, wherein categories impersonate and many devices are called into full play. But a confusion has been created by the intermingling of the isolates of V History and W Political Science. In some cases, especially the constitutional aspects of a country, it requires a meticulous mind to distinguish between the two main classes. Ranganathan has clearly explained the difference in Sec. V32 (pages 1.115-1.116) of the Rules. A theoretical aspect of constitution or a similar subject should go into W Political Science and an historical account into V History. The facet formula is

V[P], [P2] : [E] [2P] '[T]

As is obvious [T] may often be required and its focus should be as sharp as the exact year. Two different points in time (span) may be connected by any of the two arrows viz., backward arrow or forward arrow usually it is the backward arrow.

[P] is the **community** as distinguished from the geographical area. Its focus is to be got by (GD). *It means that the space isolates officiate as personality isolates.*

It may be noticed that the [P] may further be sharpened by (SID) for constructing the isolate number of the colonies of one imperialist country in other parts of the world. [P] can further be amplified by (SD) whenever necessary. Near sovereign states are got by (CD).

[P2] is the organ of the government.

[E] cum [2P] cover the activities, functions and policies of the government.

History of India
V44

History of Punjab
V4443

India from 1857 to 1947
V44 'N47 ← M57
Or
V44 'M57 → N47

(Use any arrow but make sure that the time flows from lower to the higher point).

Greek History in 500 BC
V51 'C499

History of British India
V44-56

History of French Empire in Africa
V6-53

British colonies in the 19th century
V1-56 'M

History of Hindi speaking states in India
V44(P152)

History of Feudal Europe brought upto 15th century
V5(W3) 'I

History of the Christian people of the world upto the Middle Ages
V1(Q6) 'G

Powers of the English Monarch in Feudal England
V56(W3), 1 : 3

Functions of Judiciary in European Communist Countries
V5(W691), 7 : 3

History of Princely states of Punjab brought upto 1947
V4436(W4) 'N5

Freedom of education in Catholic countries brought upto 1980s
V1 (Q62) : 58(T) 'N9

Functions of Prime Minister of India brought upto 2000s
V2, 21 : 3 'P1

Structure of Indian Legislature brought upto 1960s
V2, 3 : 2 'N7

Specific political parties may be got by (CD):

Indian National Congress
V44, 4M89

Janta Party
V44, 4N77

Bhartiya Janta Party
V44, 4N80

History of the functions of civil administration brought upto 1970s
V2, 8 : 3 'N7

Constitutional Law of India—A historical account
V2 : 2 : (Z)

A historical account of Home policy in British India brought upto 1947
V2-56 : 11 'N5

Functions of the Viceroy General of British India
V2-56, 11 : 3

Powers and functions of the UN Secretary General
V1N48, 1 : 3

V : 19 Foreign Policy presents another interesting case. It has been endowed with the status of a main class by fitting it with its own facet formula (Rule V319 page 24 of the Annexure).

V : 19 [P], [P_2]

[P] is the community to which the foreign policy is directed: to be got by (GD).

[P2] is the subject of the foreign policy to be got by (SD).

Here [P_1] and [P_2] are telescoped, so if [P_1] is absent there is no need to put comma before [P_2]. And no confusion or cluttering of facets can arise from such a rule, since [P_2] is always got by (SD) and is thus recognizable.

History of cold war between USA and USSR brought upto 1990's
V73 : 1947, (zE) 'N9

India's commercial policy towards C'wealth countries
V2 : 191N48, (X : 54)

Diplomatic relations between the Jews and Muslims brought upto 1970s
V1(Q7) : 191 (Q5), (zB) 'N7

US armament policy towards Pakistan
V73 : 1944Q7, (zS)

Cultural Relations between USSR and India
V2 : 1947, (Y : 1)

India's foreign economic policy
V2 : 19(X)

US armament policy
V73 : 19(zS)

Note that in the above two cases [P_1] is absent, and [P_2] has been attached directly.

In case of tables of political persons, the appropriate class number should be followed by s, which is further sharpened by (CD) covering the (LED).

Table of US President brought upto 2000AD
V73, 1sP1

Table of English monarchs brought upto 1952
V56, 1sN5

In case of biography of a politician or a statesman, the digit pair y7 is to be added to the community facet.

Life of Mahatma Gandhi
V2y7M69

Biography of Napoleon
V53y7L69

Philosophy of History
V : (R)

Influence of library science on archaeology
V : 710g2

A comparative study of the powers of the President and Prime Minister of Indian Republic brought upto 1970s
V44, 10m21 : 3 'N7

All India Conference on Punjab History 1980
V4436 p44, N80

Indo-African Trade Journal (India 1965+)
V44 : 196, (X : 5)m44, N6

National Archives (India)
V44 : 8, d, 9M

Report of the Indian Institute of Historical Studies
V.44, d, 9N3r

Indian Council of Historical Research (1972)
V.44,f, 9N7

Canadian Historical Association (1974)
V.72.g, 9N7

Issue of Pakistan armament in Indo-US Foreign relations
V44 : 1973, (V44Q7 : 191(zS))

Issue of Kashmir in Indo-Pak relations
V44 : 1944Q7, (V4447)

Bibliography of Persian Manuscripts on Mughal History of India
V44 'Ja12-3164

American Institute of Research in Indian History
V44 : f.73, d, 9N

39

W POLITICAL SCIENCE

To those who have learned the intricacies of V History, the W Political Science schedule presents itself as an easy case. But the difficulty of choosing between V History and W Political Science may still persist. It may be stated again that subjects treated purely from theory viewpoint are to be put in W Political Science. The facet formula is

$$W[P], [P_2] : [E] [2P]$$

[P] is the kind of state

$[P_2]$ is the organ of the state; its isolates are the same as the $[P_2]$ of the V History.

[E] cum [2P] cover activities, politics, and functions of the state. Again the isolates are the same as those of V History.

Theory of International Relations
W : 19

Powers of monarchs in limited monarchies
W46, 1 : 3

What is *laissez faire*
W : 33

Freedom of Press in India
W : 58(4).44

(Here [E] 58 has been sharpened by (SD).4 is Journalism see page 2.4)

History of Election systems of Europe brought upto 1970s
W : 91v5 'N7

Civic duties in dictatorship rule
W64 : 5

Geopolitics
W0gU

Political Sociology
Y0gW

Liberty by J.S. Mill
W : 511

Functions of Legislature in world state
W95, 3 : 3

Utopian State Laissez-faire
W7 : 33

Democratic monarchy
W40k6

Difference between representative democracy and direct democracy
W610w2

Indian Journal of Political Science (1940)
Wm44, N4

Raj Vidya (1964+)
Wm44, N6

Journal of International Politics, USA
W : 19m73, N

Indian Association of Political Science
W.44,g,9N

40

X ECONOMICS

In the CC, X Economics includes transport, commerce, taxation, international trade, industries, labour problems, production, consumption, office and personnel management. Systems and Specials also occur which have been listed at the end, as usual. The facet formula in ultimate is:

X (System), (Special), [P] ; [M] : [E] [2P]

[P] is the business

[M] is the medium of currency. It is a **differential facet** applicable only to X61 Money.

[E] cum [2P] covers the economic problems and activities.

It may be noticed that some isolates such as Transport, Commerce, etc., occur both in [P] and [E]. In such a case, in [P] should be put the business aspect, while in [E] should be put the method, techniques and other such problems.

In case of Industrial Economics X8 [P]8 should be further sharpened by (SD) for any specific industry.

Standard of Living in India
X : 16.44

Value of Gold Currency in Japan
X61 ; 1 : 7.42

X62 and X72 have their own respective special energy isolates, given at the end of the general energy isolates of X, at page 2.114, column second.

Rate of interest in commercial banks
X625 : 11

Progressive property taxation
X722 : 13

Equal taxation system in India
X72 : 11.44

Paper export
X8(M13) : 545

Marketing of published material
X8(M16) : 51

Economic conditions in the Muslim countries in 21st century
X.1(Q7) 'P

Demand and Supply Theory
X : 73

Mathematics of Demand-Supply equation
X : 73 : (B)

Any specific theory of Demand and Supply may be got by (CD)—treating it a system.

Say's Law of Demand and Supply
X : 73M

Various theories of demand
X : 731A

Office Management
X : 8M

Indian Law for advertising tobacco products
X8(J452) : 513 : (Z44)

Wages in publishing industry
X8(M16) : 93

Wages in small scale publishing concerns
X9B, 8(M16) : 93

Wages in small scale publishing concerns in cooperative economy
XM, 9B, 8(M16) : 93

Trade Unions in large scale textile mills in technocracy
XN19, 9D, 8(M7) : 97D

Eccentricity of X Economics schedules lies in dividing X : 9 Personnel Management into, what Ranganathan calls, three sectors categorized as follows:

(1) X : 9 to X : 9915
(least concrete sector of X : 9)
(2) X : 99A to X : 99W
(More concrete sector of X : 9)
(3) X : 9A to X : 9Q
(Still more concrete sector of X : 9)

If a subject is such that its isolates lie in more than one sector, then the latter sector should form the earlier level and the common digits are not to be repeated in the latter levels; the levels are to be separated by a comma.

Wages in Cycle Industry
X8(D5125) : 93

Female workers in cycle industry
X8(D5125) : 9F

Wages of female workers in cycle industry
X8(D5125) : 9F, 3

Since in the above example X:9F Female workers lies in the still more concrete sector, while wages X:93 lies in the least concrete sector of 9, so X:9F forms the earlier level. And since the digit 9 is common to both the sectors, so it is not to be repeated in the latter level.

Wages of female workers in Public sector cycle industry in socialist economy
XM2, 9W, 8(D5125) : 9F, 3

Working hours of seasonal unskilled labour in tea plantations
X8(J451) : 9G5, 9C, 55

Wages of agricultural semi-skilled war refugees
XB, 8(J) : 9J4, 9D, 3

Social security for clerical female workers in a public enterprise
X9W : 9F, 9P, 58

Job evaluation of part-time research workers in dye and paint industry
X8(F58) : 9G4, 9R, 1

Similarly X:97 Industrial Relations has been divided into three sectors. Therefore, a subject of industrial relations which covers more than one sector of X:97, the latter sector should form the earlier level.

Settlement in strike by trade unions
X : 97D, 9D, 8

Moral maintenance in lock-out of a textile industry
X8(M7) : 979W, 1

Arbitration in the industrial dispute of coal miners
X8(F551) : 979C, 6

Settlement in the strike by medical staff
X8(L) : 979D, 8

Settlement in the strike of married female workers
X : 9F5, 79D, 8

Medical facilities for rural semi-skilled labour in Tea Plantation of Assam
X8(J451) : 9H1, 9D, 5854.4477

(In the above case the levels 1 and 2 have the digit 9 in common, while in levels 2 and 3, the digits 97 are common. Common digits have not been repeated).

Settlement in the strike of supervisory seasonal staff of a forest in Communistic economy
XN, 8(JB): 9G5, 9G, 79D, 8

(It is a mixed case: the first two levels belong to X:9 while the last two levels belong to X:97. But all the three sectors of X:97 fall in the least concrete sector of X:9).

Computer industry in India
X8(D65, 8(B)).44

Marketing of Cosmetic products in China
X8(F95) : 51.41

Marketing of Academic library services
X8(23 : 7) : 51

Law of Alcohol advertisement in India
X8(F54) : 513 : (Z44)

Import of mechanical translation equipment in India
X8(D6, 8(P : 795)) : 546.44

Trade relations between India and USA
X : 5.440j73
(Intra-Facet general relation)

India's preference in marketing agricultural produce towards Africa
X8(J) : 51.440k6

Pakistan's preference in exporting wheat towards Muslim countries
X8(J382) : 545.4470k 1 (Q7)

Influence of banking in public finance in a Communistic economy
XN, 7 or 6

Difference between accountancy and audits
X:8 H0wJ

It is a case of Intra-array Difference phase Relation

(The phase relation symbol w will indicate that here J is a part of 8, instead of being a Main class agriculture).

Indian Journal of Agricultural Economy (1950+)
X8(J)m44, N5

Journal of Mathematical Economics, (1924+), (the Netherlands)
X : (B)m5962, N7

History of Political Economy (USA, 1973+) : A Journal
Xvm73, N7

Statistical Abstract (India) (Annual)
X8(A) : 2.44sN

A survey for Cosmetics Market in India
X8(F95) : 51 : u

Advertising profession in India
X : 513.44, b

Indian Railways
X415.44, w, 9M

Indian Society for Agricultural Economists (1939)
X8(J).44, g, 9N3

International Labour Organization (ILO) (1919)
X:9.1, w, 9N19

(It has been treated as a government department)

Indian Bureau of Weights and Measures (1946)
X : 5c.44, w, 9N46

For weights and measures, the class number is
X : 5c (Rule X : 9e page 1.119)

Indian Institute of Management (Calcutta)
X : 8.44.C, e4, I

(It has been treated as a local institution)

Indian Institute of Economic Growth
X.44, e4, 9N5

Indian Institute of Chartered Accountants (1949)
X:8F.44, d, 9N49

Golden Arrow Transporters, Amritsar
X411.4443.A, k, G

Indian Economic Association (1918)
X.44, g, 9N18

Great European Economists, Youngest born in 1882
Xw5, M9

Ten great economists (youngest born in 1905)
XwN1

Life of Lord Keynes (1883-1946)
XwM83

Bibliography of Agricultural Labour in India (1975)
X8(J) : 9aN7

Bureau of Indian Standards (1947)
X:5e.44, d, 9N4

Das Kapital
XM2x1, 1

(It has been got by Claesic Device)

41

Y SOCIOLOGY

Science of society which deals with the collective behaviour of socially organized groups. In the CC, Y Sociology also includes social work, culture, civilization and anthropology. Here [2E] cum [3P] facet also occurs. The facet formula is

Y[P] : [E][2P] : [2E] [3P]

[P] is the community or social group-isolates enumerated.

[P] isolates can further be sharpened by (SID), (GD) and (SD).

[E] cum [2P] facet covers activities, traditions, social problems.

Device of parallel schedules has been used frequently.

[2E] cum [3P] : Secondary problems. It includes conservation, development, etiology, prevention and correction of social ills. It may be noted that [E] 4 isolates have their own different [2E] cum [3P] isolates.

It may be reminded that [2E] cum [3P] cannot exist without the prior existence of [E] cum [2P]. Therefore, whether stated explicitly or not [E] must be supplied whenever [2E] facet occurs.

A social study of urban women
Y15-33

Prevention of social evils among the slum youth
Y12-57 : 44 : 5

Educating the slum-youth against social evils
Y12-57 : 44 : 5(T)

Flood relief work in Orissa in 1997
Y : 4355 : 67.4471 'N97

Relief work for the Earthquake victims of Gujarat in 2001
Y : 436 : 67.4436 'P01

Urban families of India—a social study
Y33 : 32.44

3[E] has been sub-divided as R4 Ethics

Coronation Ceremony of a British Monarch
Y756 : 348(W, 21)

Here Y7 has been divided by (GD)

Inauguration ceremony of a rural public library
Y31 : 348(22)

Aryan Civilization
Y73(P1) : 1

Indus Valley Civilization in 3500 BC
Y : 1.44.g11 'B6499

Naming ceremony of Hindu children
Y73(Q2) : 3411

Superstitions about devils among the Christians
Y73(Q6) : 35412

Here Y : 354 has been sub-divided as [P_2] of Mysticism

Sky in Dravidian Folklore
Y73(P3) : 35128

Here note the double borrowing in the energy isolate 35128; first from [P_2] of Δ Mysticism and then from [P3] of ND Sculpture.

Moon in Dravidian Folkore
Y73(P3) : 351282

Here the borrowing has been triple: first from [P_2] of Δ, then [P_2] of ND. and lastly from [P] of B9.

Superstitions about earthquakes among the Hindus
Y73(Q2) : 354(H4132)

Arm ornaments of Stone Age
Y714 : 8663

Here Y:86 has been subdivided as 1[P] of L Medicine.

Earrings worn by Asians
Y74 : 8683

Mining instruments of the Jews
Y73(Q5) : 83(HZ)

Medical instruments of the Semitic people
Y73(P2) : 83(L)

Water boats of the primitive Australians
Y72-78 : 852

A social study of suicides among the wives in Europe
Y2215 : 45111.5

Social life of Doctors
Y9(L)

Alcoholism among the Musicians
Y9(NR) : 411

Rural Development
Y31 : 7 : 7

Character improvement
Y : 74 : 7

Women empowerment in 21st Century
Y15 : 7 : 7 'P

Etiology of overpopulation in India
Y : 52 : 2.44

Population control by legislation
Y : 5 : 5(Z)

A social study of war crimes in Bangladesh
Y : 45ZA. 44Q71

(Y:45 has been sub-divided as Z, 5 crimes, where Z, 5ZA is war crimes Law).

Influence of overpopulation on crimes—a social study
Y : 45 0r52

Difference between the population densities of rural and urban areas
Y310w3 : 58

Guru Nanak Journal of Sociology (India, 1980+)
Ym44, N80

Indian Sociological Bulletin (1963+)
Ym44, N63

Sociological Abstracts
Yam73, N

Journal of Marriage and Family (US, 1938+)
Y2m73, N3

The Netherlands Sociological Society, 1963
Y.5952, g, 9N6

National Institute of Rural Development, Hyderabad 1958
Y31 : 7 : 7.44, d, 9N5

Distribution of Anglo-Indian population
Y594-73(P15)-756 : 58

Social Relief work to Pak War Prisoners in 1971 in India
Y744Q7 : 4(Z, A, 6) : 67.44 'N71

42

Z LAW

Law of a particular subject such as library legislation, public health law, law of passports, according to the CC, are classed with their respective subjects. Here personality occurs in four levels. The facet formula is:

Z[P], [P_2], [P_3], [P_4] : [E] [2P]

It may be noted that here comma is present between [P_2] and [P_3] while usually it is absent.

[P] is the community over which a given law has the jurisdiction. It is got by (GD) in case of a nation, and by (SD) in case of a cultural community. *But it should be noted carefully that [P] stands for community and not the subject.*

[P_2] and [P_3] have been termed as Law I and Law II respectively. In case of [P_2] A War Law, all the earlier isolates of [P_2] are applicable after Z, A and its subdivision, viz., Z, B Z, C and Z, D.

[P_3] isolates vary according to [P_2]. Therefore there is no general schedule of [P_3] isolates. Similarly [P_4] isolates are only applicable to Z, 7, 7. Judgement and decree.

[E] cum [2P] cover the problems of Z, 98 Legal Documents.

Indian Law
Z44

Muslim Law
Z(Q7)

International Law
Z1

International Law of Japan
Z42

International Law of Libels
Z1, 572

International Law of War
Z1, A

International War Law of Arms
Z1, A264

Succession in US copyright law
Z73, 2674, 6

Punjab Law of Local Bodies Jurisdiction
Z4443, 186, 1

Divorce Law
Z, 835

Ultra vires in Muslim Divorce Law
Z(Q7), 1227, 15

Punjab Land Ceiling Act, 1972
Z4443, 211, 14 'N72

Hindu Law of Oral Contract
Z(Q2), 3, 21

Hindu Succession Act, 1956
Z(Q2), 2, 6 'N56

[P_2] 4, 5, 6, 91, 92, 93 and 95 have no [P_3]; only Z, 94 and its subdivisions have [P_4] isolates).

Ex parte summary trials in Pakistan Law
Z44Q7, 751, 73

Indian Law of session case award partition
Z44, 755, 75, 2

Registrar of the High Court of J & K
Z4447, 83, 81

Weightage given to the direct evidence
Z, 9414, 3

Drafting of negotiable instruments
Z, 985:1

Indian Law of cancellation of deeds
Z44, 981:5

Sacred sources of Jewish Law
Z(Q5), 921

Civil procedures in summary trials
Z, 751, 11

Indian law of pre-emption of property
Z44, 2, 195

To repeat again if, [P_2] is A, B, C or D, War Law, then all the earlier subdivisions of [P_2] are applicable after A, B, C and D. In such cases [P_2] isolates have their own separate [P_3] isolates—applicable to War Law. It is yet another case of differential facets.

Law of War prisoners
Z1, A, 6

Evidence in War Law
Z, A94

Law of Summary trials in land war
Z, B751

International Law of declaration of Sea War
Z1, C, 1

US War Law of mines
Z73, A2113

US War Law of mine invasion
Z73, A2113, 31

Summary trials of War prisoners
Z, A751, 6

A comparative study of Indian and British Property ownership laws
Z440m56, 2, 1

Difference between slavery and forced labour according to Indian law
Z44, 512620w3

Difference between immovable and movable property according to law of sea war
Z, C210n6

Indian law for abetment of war crimes
Z44, 5ZA04

British law for abetment in crimes against religion
Z56, 5Q04

Pakistan law of crime against Muslim religion
Z44Q7, 5Q7

All India Conference on International Law, 1978
Z1p44, N78

Journal of Indian Law Institute (1958+)
Zm44, N5

A periodical reporting law cases should be fitted with two (ACI)s in succession namely "y7m".

Summary of Recent Decisions relating to Law of Real Property (USA, 1936+)
Z73, 2y7mN3 oR Z73, Zy7m73, N3

Indian Law Reporter (1967+)
Z44ymN6 or Z44y7m44, N6

In the above two examples, [P_1] of the (ACI) digit m may be avoided if desired as it has already been represented in the class numbers.

Supreme Court Weekly Reporter (1963)
Z44, 81y7mN6 or Z44, 81y7m44, N6

Indian Institute of International Law (1964)
Z1.44, d, 9N6

Indian Law Institute (1956)
Z.44, d, 9N5

National Law University, Hyderabad
Z.44, e4, 9N

President of the Supreme Court Bar Association of India
Z44, 81, 5, g, 9N, 1

43

BOOK NUMBER AND CALL NUMBER

Documents embody knowledge. Classification of documents though is based on their contents, viz., knowledge, but the oddities and realities of the physical body of the documents cannot be ignored. In a library one cannot classify distinctively without also accounting for these physical peculiarities. Therefore, it is generally seen that the class number alone fails to individualise a book in a library or in a bibliography. Many books in a library may get the same class number by virtue of having the same specific subject. In such cases to assign a unique individual place to a given document—as it is the requirement of every library—these documents are given a further notation, also called **External Notation**. This external notation based on some non-subject considerations, used to arrange documents within a given specific subject, is known as a Book Number. **Function of a book number starts where that of a class number ends**. Book number may be based on either one or all of the considerations such as author, title, edition, language, physical form or the year of publication or even the place of publication. Supplement, concordance, volume, or copy numbers too may have to be considered.

In many schemes of classification and consequently in libraries book numbers get only insignificant treatment—even stepmotherly behaviour. Not only this, many schemes are silent on the issue. Therefore, it has prompted classifier to use any locally devised arbitrary method of giving book numbers. Like his classification system his book number system too is faceted. In the facet formula of book number Ranganathan has provided even obscure and rarely occurring elements in book numbers. Besides the year of publication, his book number takes notice of language, form, volume number, supplement, copy number and critical commentary, if any. The colon book number facet formula along with the indicator digits is:

[L] [F] [Y] [A]. [V]-[S]; [C]: g[EVN]

wherein

L	—	Language of the document.
F	—	Form of the document.
Y	—	Year of publication of the document.
A	—	Accession part of the year number.
V	—	Volume number of the document.
S	—	Supplement number of the document.
C	—	Copy number of the document.
g	—	Evaluation Number
EVN	—	Accession part of the evaluation number.

Apparently it looks that the formula is quite complex and the resulting book number would be quite lengthy. Far from this, in practice the CC book number is very simple and brief; and it is estimated that about 90 per cent of the book numbers consist of only two digits for the year number. Other facets are only occasionally geared into service.

Position and role of various facets in the book number formula are as follows.

[L] *Language Facet*

It is worth noting that the first characteristic to subdivide a given specific class is the language. So, in this way all the documents in one language within a given class come together. Since most of the library users are monolingual, they find together at one place all the books in their language. This saves their time.

The language isolates are the same as meant for the general CC schedule [as given on pages 2.26-2.27 (Chapter 5) (CC-6)]. In many cases, as enumerated below, the **language number is omitted:**

(a) There is no need of language facet for books in the favoured language of the library. Favoured language of the library is either the mother-tongue or the official language. For example, in India, English is the favoured language in majority of the libraries. Since the majority of the books in the library are in the favoured language, so most of the books will not need this facet. This makes for brevity and simplicity of the book number.

(b) Book Numbers for books in the main classes Literature and Linguistics do not require the language facet as the language number is already present in the class number, and as such it will be superfluous to repeat it. However, in cases of *language* *inequality*. The language facet in book number many be needed.*

(c) Lastly the language facet may be omitted from the book number of serial/periodical publications.

[F] *Form Facet*

The form facet represents the way of presentation of the subject in the document. It is what Ranganathan calls the subtle body of the document. For example, a book may be all pictures; another may be a practical book; yet another may be merely a tabulated data. List of forms can be multiplied and in this age of information many new forms of documents are being invented and introduced. Isolate numbers, consisting of Roman small usually followed by an Indo-Arabic numeral have been enlisted on page 2.3 (Chapter 02) of CC-6 (1963). That list is not exhaustive. However, the **Form number is omitted** in the books which are in the favoured form of the library. In a general library printed cuboid books in prose make the favoured Form category. Hence majority of the books are without this facet, too. For example, a book on economic progress through "graphs" will get the form facet 'h' in book number and a lecture will get the facet number p 1 in book number.

[Y] *Year Facet*

This is the indispensable facet, as no Colon Book Number is without it. This facet denotes the year of publication of the book. For this purpose, Ranganathan has designed a special chronological table from 1880 to 2119 to turn out brief isolate numbers of this facet. This table, given at page 1.13 of CC-6, 1963, is as follows:

A	Before 1880	J	1950-1959
B	1880-1889	K	1960-1969
C	1890-1899	L	1970-1979
D	1990-1909	M	1980-1989
E	1910-1919	N	1990-1999
F	1920-1929	P	2000-2009
G	1930-1939	Q	2010-2019
H	1940-1949	R	2020-2029

* Language inequality is a situation when a book on literature or linguistics is written in other than its original language. For example, Shakespeare in Hindi or French, for that reason in any language other than English in a case of language inequality. Similarly, a book on French grammar or history of Spanish language written, say, in English are another cases of language inequality.

S	2030-2039	X	2080-2089
T	2040-2049	Y	2090-2099
U	2050-2059	ZA	2100-2109
V	2060-2069	ZB	2110-2119
W	2070-2079		

In the Table every digit from B onwards spans a decade; and a particu!ar year is denoted by adding the year number of that decade to the decade digit. For example 1987 is M7, 1969 is K9, 2000 is P0 and 2005 is P05. Therefore a book on Lectures on Economics published in 1975 will be p1L5; and a book on Lectures on Economics in Hindi in 1975 will be 153 p1L5.

Similarly the book number for a document published in 1983 in film form in Russian language will be

142 f953L3

where 142 is Russian language, f953 is film, L3 is 1973

[A] ***Accession Part of the Year Number***

This is a device to distinguish more than one book published in the same year, language and form in a given specific subject. This consists in adding 1, 2, 3, etc., for the 2nd, 3rd, 4th, etc., to the year number of the book number. For example, the first book on Physics published in 1987 will have the class number M7; and the second will have M71; and the 3rd, M72 and so on. Again, let us say, in 1963 several books on the history of Hindi literature were published. All will have the class number O152v. Their book numbers in order will be:

K3	for the 1st book
K31	for the 2nd book
K32	for the 3rd book
K33	for the 4th book
K3n-1	for the nth book

This device is not much used except in a very current topic say, computers, environment today.

[V] ***Volume Number of the Document***

Many books especially the reference books and other source documents are completed in many volumes. Quite obviously all the volumes of a 'book' need to be placed together. To do this, Ranganathan suggests to put 1, 2, 3, etc., for the first, second and third volume, etc., after the accession part of the year number facet. Volume Number is preceded by a dot (.). Suppose we have a book Palgrave's *Dictionary of Economics* in 3 Volumes published in 1987. Each volume will have the book number:

M7.1	1st Volume
M7.2	2nd Volume
M7.3	3rd Volume

[S] *Supplement Number of the Document*

Sometimes it happens that to update a book, or to correct the earlier one, or to add some latest development in the field, a supplement to original book is issued. Sometimes more than one supplement may be issued successively. The need to keep together the original and the supplements is pretty obvious. A supplement separated from its original book is like a child lost in a fair. So, to keep the host and the associated book together Ranganathan prescribed a symbol hyphen (-) followed by the supplement Number. In the formula it comes after the Volume [V] facet. The supplement will bear the year number [Y] of the original book, and not the actual year of its publication. Let us say, a book published in 1982 has two supplements issued in 1983 and 1987. Their book numbers will respectively be:

M2	Original Book
M2-1	1st supplement
M2-2	2nd supplement

If the book is multivolumed then the supplement is placed after the last volume unless specified otherwise. The supplement number will be:

M2.1	1st volume
M2.2	2nd volume
M2.2-1	1st supplement (1983)
M2.2-2	2nd supplement (1987)

It is a simple but very effective device.

[C] *Copy Number of the Document*

It usually happens that a book is acquired in multiple copies by a particular library. In academic libraries textbooks are usually required in multiple copies. So, all these books will have to be kept together in a given section of the library. To keep all these copies together Ranganathan provided a copy number facet in the formula. It is positioned after the supplement number and its indicator digit is semicolon (;). The first copy will have no copy number and the second copy will be indicated as; '1' and so on. For example a book published in Urdu on Indian history published in 1987 has 10 copies. All of them will have the class number V44 or 954 and their book numbers will be:

168M7	1st copy
168M7;1	2nd copy
168M7;2	3rd copy
168M7;9	10th copy

[:g] ***Criticism/Evaluation Number***

This is analogous to the Energy Posteriorising Common isolate (PCI) of the Colon Classification though here it is applied to the book number and not to the class number. There are some non-classical books having a semblance of a classic. It is imperative to keep a book and its various commentaries or evaluations together. This is done by adding ':g' to the last facet of the book number. For example, if a book published in 1980 has its commentary published in 1983, their book number will be as follows:

M0	For Original Book
M0:g	First Commentary published in 1983

It will keep the parental book and its sequel/commentaries together.

[EVN] ***Accession Part of the Evaluation Number***

This works exactly as [A] does for [Y]. The [EVN] is only to distinguish one commentary from the other and is done by adding 1, 2, 3, etc., to ':g' for the 2nd, 3rd and 4th commentary respectively.

So, for the above book

M0:g1	2nd commentary
M0:g2	3rd commentary
M0:g3	4th commentary
M0:g4	5th commentary, and so on.

Problems

So far so good. However this facet formula is not without problems. For example, it is not able to keep together all the books of the same author on one subject. This is a minor problem compared to another problem of keeping together the different editions of a book. Since different editions are published in different years, each edition will have the book number based on the year of its publication and hence get separated. For example, let us say, a book first published in 1968 was issued in 2nd edition in 1975. Their book numbers respectively will be:

K 8
L 5

and these 'two' books will get separated by many intervening books published between 1968 and 1975. Hence the problem. But Ranganathan has not been oblivious of the problem. At the first instance, Ranganathan does not consider it necessary to keep the different editions of a book together. To him it serves no purpose. However, to those insisting on keeping together these editions, Ranganathan suggests that an edition may be treated as a copy of the first edition. For example, in the above case the second edition will get the book number:

K8 ; L5

So, if this book has another edition, say, in 1984 it may have the book number:

K8 ; M4

Thus the three editions will have the book numbers:

K8	1st edition
K8 ; L5	2nd edition
K8 ; M4	3rd edition

Hence the three editions will get juxtaposed. This method, however, is not a neat solution to the problem as the latter editions are out of their chronological place. Despite these minor problems, Ranganathan's is still the most developed Book Number yet formulated. One great advantage of Ranganathan's system and for that reason of any chronological Book Number is that these are applicable to all the documents irrespective of the language, script or the cultural or ethnic origin of the author.

Collection Number

In the art of library classification the first division of books does not take into consideration the subject matter. Every big library is a cluster of parallel libraries, i.e., libraries within a library. Parallel libraries are called sections. The first consideration is the section to which it should go. We first determine whether the book under classification is a rare book, manuscript, thesis, textbook, reference book or any special collection book. These sections may be dictated by the utilitarian purpose such as reference or a textbook or for the convenience of managing them such as abnormal sized book, rarebooks and so on. Thus in a library there are many mini libraries within a given library.

The symbol determining the section of the book preceding the class number is termed as the collection number. Putting the symbol for the collection number seems so simple and obvious that no scheme other than the CC has discussed it in an academic way. Here the collection number has been designed in relation to the book number; in many cases the collection number is denoted by adding some indicator digit to the book number. While in some cases—mostly utility oriented—a separate symbol is added for the collection number. It may be any arbitrary symbol, but usually the initials of the section name:

R	Reference
RR	Rare book
T	Thesis
Tx	Text
G	Government publication
RP	Reports

If it is a departmental library, Ranganathan suggests the following convention:

BD	Mathematics Department
DD	Engineering Department
LD	Medical College
RD	Philosophy Department
YD	Sociology Department
ZD	Law Department

But for the abnormal books Ranganathan enumerates the following rules:

Underline the book number for	small sized books
Overline the book number for	large sized books
Both underline and overline the book number for	abnormal books

Encircle the book number for worn out books.*

Since each symbol creates its own section, so no ordinal value of these digits has been fixed. These sections may be located at convenience. The most general collection is not given any collection number—application of the **favoured category principle**.

The combination of collection number, class numbers, and the book number when taken together in the above sequence is termed as the **call number**. The equation is :

Call Number = Collection Number + Class Number + Book Number

* Here enclosing the above number between parentheses seems more easy and tidy.

It is the call number which determines the specific and unique place of a document in the library.

Using CC Book Numbers with other Schemes

It is not necessary that only the libraries using Colon Classification can use this book number system. Libraries using different schemes such as DDC, UDC., LC, or Bliss' Bibliographic classification can use these book numbers with equal ease and effectiveness. But in such cases some adaptation will have to be made. Sometimes what Ranganathan has included in the Book Numbers is made a part of class numbers in other systems. Form of a book is a standard subdivision in the DDC; and in UDC language of the book is accounted for in the class numbers. Therefore, in such case the CC book numbers will have to be adapted accordingly.

REFERENCES

1. For explanation of this term, see Satija, M.P., *Manual of Practical Colon Classification*, New Delhi: Sterling, 1984, p. 83.
2. Letters I and O have not been used.

FURTHER READINGS

1. Satija, M.P., *A Primer on Ranganathan Book Number*, New Delhi: Mittal Publications, 1987, pp. xvii, 87.
   This work explains Ranganathan's book number in all its details, ramifications and intricacies. The text has been illustrated with ample examples. This is a simple and systematic exposition of the theory and practice of book numbers developed by Ranganathan, International *Classification*, 15(2), p. 102 Cochrane A. Pauline, 1989.
2. Satija, M.P. and Comaromi, John P., *Beyond Classification: Book Numbers*, New Delhi: Ess Ess, 1992, pp. 60-78.
3. Satija, M.P., "Book Number and Call Number" in *Encyclopedia of Library and Information Science*, ed. by Allen Kent, New York: Marcel Dekker, 1990, Vol. 45, pp. 18-45.

INDEX